AF471855

LETTERS

ON

AMERICAN SLAVERY,

ADDRESSED TO

MR. THOMAS RANKIN,

Merchant at Middlebrook, Augusta Co., Va.

BY JOHN RANKIN,

Pastor of the Presbyterian Churches of Ripley and Strait-Creek, Brown County, Ohio.

FIFTH EDITION.

BOSTON:

PUBLISHED BY ISAAC KNAPP.

25 CORNHILL.

1838.

This book has been printed "on demand" and is therefore environmentally sustainable. There is no waste from excessive or unnecessary printing nor any energy spent in pulping unsold copies.

ISBN: 978-1-967254-10-1

Foreword to this New Edition

When Rev. John Rankin first penned his Letters on American Slavery in the 1820s and 1830s, he did so not with the distance of a scholar or the detachment of a politician, but with the burning conviction of a man of faith—a minister and father unwilling to remain silent as human beings were bought, sold, and brutalized under the sanction of American law and culture.

Writing to his brother in the slaveholding South, Rankin laid out an uncompromising moral argument against slavery grounded in the teachings of Scripture, the claims of conscience, and the founding ideals of the American republic.

Rankin's voice was a prophetic one—not only because he called his nation to account, but because he did so before it was fashionable or safe to do so. His house in Ripley, Ohio, became a station on the Underground Railroad, and his moral clarity helped inspire others, including William Lloyd Garrison and Frederick Douglass.

Nearly two centuries later, Letters on American Slavery still speaks—both as a historical document and a moral compass. Rankin's urgent appeal to his brother—to see the humanity of the enslaved and to act in faith—is a timeless reminder that silence in the face of oppression is complicity.

We invite you not only to learn from Rev. Rankin's words but to be challenged by them. His arguments were rooted not in partisanship or politics, but in the belief that justice, if it is to mean anything, must be lived out—publicly, sacrificially, and without fear.

These letters are not relics of a bygone era. They are calls to action for ours.

July 2025

Yours Truly
John Rankin

PREFACE.

The following Letters were originally designed for the benefit of the Brother to whom they were addressed. For his convenience they were inserted in the Castigator, and by that means were first brought to public view.

The solicitations of a few friends, in connection with the desire of aiding and encouraging every effort for the liberation of the enslaved and degraded Africans, were the means of bringing them before the public a second time, and in another form.

They have received several alterations and additions. And some efforts have been made to render the work more complete than it was in its original form; but still, it is far from possessing that excellence of composition which the importance of its subject requires. Therefore, it is desired that its imperfections may be attributed to the weakness of its author, and not to that of the cause it is intended to support.

But little can reasonably be hoped in relation to the success of this work, when it is considered that, in addition to the difficulties arising from its own imperfections, it must bear the charge of fanaticism, and contend with prejudices that have been rapidly increasing for ages. In opposition to it, more than ten thousand envenomed tongues, and pens dipt in the gall of unrelenting avarice, may be expected to plead the cause of injustice.

These difficulties, however, should be considered as so many arguments in favor of the work. If but a little good can be done, it is the more necessary that that little should be done. That involuntary slavery is a very dangerous evil, and that our nation is involved in it, none can, with truth, deny. And that the safety of our government, and the happiness of its subjects, depend upon the extermination of this evil, must be obvious to every enlightened mind. Nor is it less evident, that it is the duty of every citizen, according to his station, talents and opportunity, to use suitable exertions for the abolition of an evil which is pregnant with the growing principles of ruin. Surely, no station should be unimproved, no talent, however small, should be buried; nor should any opportunity of doing good be lost, when the safety of a vast nation, and the happiness of millions of the human family, demand prompt and powerful exertions. Everything that can be done, either by fair discussion, or by any other lawful means, ought to be done, and done speedily, in order to avert the hastening ruin that must otherwise soon overtake us!

Let all the friends of justice and suffering humanity, do what little they can, in their several circles, and according to their various stations, capacities and opportunities; and all their little streams of exertion will, in process of time, flow together, and constitute a mighty river that shall sweep away the yoke of oppression, and purge our nation from the abominations of slavery.

LETTERS ON SLAVERY.

LETTER I.

My dear Brother:

I received yours of the 2d December, with mingled sensations of pleasure and pain; it gave me pleasure to hear of your health, and pain to hear of your purchasing slaves. I consider involuntary slavery a never-failing fountain of the grossest immorality, and one of the deepest sources of human misery; it hangs like the mantle of night over our republic, and shrouds its rising glories. I sincerely pity the man who tinges his hand in the unhallowed thing that is fraught with the tears, and sweat, and groans, and blood of hapless millions of innocent, unoffending people.

A mistaken brother, who has manifested to me a kind and generous heart, claims my strongest sympathies. When I see him involved in what is both sinful and dangerous, shall I not strive to liberate him? Does he wander from the paths of rectitude, and shall not fraternal affection pursue, and call him from the verge of ruin and the unperceived precipice of wo, to the fair and pleasant walks of piety and peace? Shall I suffer sin upon my brother? No — his kindness to me forbids it, fraternal love forbids it, and what is still more to be regarded, the law of God forbids it. Though he has wandered for the moment, may I not hope to show him his error, and restrain his wanderings?

Under such views and feelings, I have resolved to address you, in a series of letters, on the injustice of enslaving the Africans. This I hope you will receive as an expression of fraternal affection, as well as of gratitude to you for former favors. I entreat you to give me that candid attention which the fondness of a brother solicits, and the importance of the subject demands. In the commencement I think it proper to apprise you that several things, connected with the present condition of the Africans, tend to bias the mind against them, and consequently incapacitate it for an impartial decision with respect to their rights.

I. Their color is very different from our own. This leads many to conclude that Heaven has expressly marked them out for servitude; and when the mind once settles upon such a conclusion, it is completely fortified against the strongest arguments that reason can suggest, or the mind of man invent. In order to save you from a conclusion so false and unreasonable, let me invite your attention to the book of inspiration; there you will find that the blackness of the African is not the horrible mark of Cain, nor the direful effects of Noah's curse, but the mark of a scorching sun. '*Look not upon me because I am black, because the sun hath looked upon me: my mother's children were angry with me; they made me the keeper of the vineyards.*' Canticles i. 6. In this passage the Church of Christ evidently speaks of herself under the figure of an Ethiopian, on whom the sun had looked with such intensity as changed his color, and so rendered him the object of hatred to the rest of mankind, who with himself originally sprang from the same mother, and were in reality his brethren. The text may be thus paraphrased. Look not upon me (with indignation) because I am black; because the sun hath looked upon me (so as to make me black) my mother's children were angry with me. This conveys, evidently, the true meaning of the passage, and shows that the Divine Spirit by whom it was dictated, assumed it as a correct principle, that the blackness of the Ethiopian's skin is caused by the sun. The word Ethiopian, which is frequently found in Scripture, denotes, according to its derivation, a person whose visage is changed to blackness by burning. The same truth is evident from the face of the world, which exhibits various shades of human color, according to all its variegated climates.

'To prove that color is the effect of climate it is only necessary to attend to certain facts which are notorious to the slightest observation.

'Geographers have divided our earth into five zones — the torrid, two temperate, and two frigid zones. The torrid zone, extending 23 1-2 degrees on each side of the equator, forms a belt of 47 degrees, running from east to west quite round the globe; to every part of which the sun is vertical at least once in the year. The ancients supposed that this region was not habitable, in consequence of the intense heat of a vertical sun. In this they were mistaken. It is found supporting, in general, as dense a population as either of the temperate zones, which lie between it and the polar circles; with, however, this remarkable difference — its inhabitants are black, or approaching to black. As this zone in its whole breadth sweeps over the continent of Africa, it embraces most of its inhabitants, who are consequently black or nearly so. As we recede from the equator toward the poles, the complexion of the inhabitants becomes gradually lighter, until in the extremities of the temperate and in the frigid zones, which lie around the poles, they are white.

'Such is the fact. And this fact alone, were we unable in the slightest degree to account for it, ought to be sufficient to satisfy the honest inquirer after truth, that color is the effect of climate. But the fact may be, we apprehend, in some degree at least, accounted for. Various anatomical experiments prove, beyond all contradiction, that the human skin consists of two lamina or coats, which are in all cases white; and that the color depends on a coagulated substance which lies between those coats. The exterior coat, being transparent and exceedingly porous, permits the sun's rays to act upon the coagulated substance freely; which, in every instance, if the action be sufficiently protracted, gives a tinge or coloring proportioned to the intensity of the sun's heat.

'To this it may be objected, that the color of the inhabitants of the several countries of our globe is not invariably the same in both parallels. This is admitted; but the objection, when examined, goes to establish our position. It is well known that the intensity of the sun's heat depends much on the nature of the earth's surface. From a smooth, level surface, the power of reflection is much greater than it is on a broken and irregular surface; and it has long been remarked, that the inhabitants of the level, sandy countries of Africa, are much blacker than those of the hilly and mountainous parts.

'And no matter what the original complexion of the emigrants to any country may have been, it is always found to accommodate itself to the hue peculiar to that country or climate. Hence the Jews, who were doubtless originally all of the same complexion, and who never intermarry with the nations among whom they sojourn, are found to be white in Germany and Poland, swarthy in Spain and Portugal, olive in the Barbary States and in Egypt, and black in Hindoostan. And hence a colony of Ethiopians, who settled at Colchis, on the Black Sea, two thousand years ago, have now become white, and the Portuguese who settled two hundred years since on the coast of Africa, black.

'But still we are asked, "If color be the effect of climate, why the negroes born in the United States are not white?" We answer, various reasons may be given. Though we are in a great measure ignorant of the economy of nature, yet we see that the complexion as well as the form of the body is propagated from father to son, and that any change which takes place in either form or complexion, must be effected by the tardy but certain operation of natural causes. We know also that it is an established law of nature, that it is much easier to communicate a *stain* than to purge it away. Hence we frequently see a swarthy hue contracted by boatmen and sailors in a few months, which it requires years to remove.

'It should moreover be recollected, that ours is not the country of white men naturally — and that, as has already been remarked, the color natural to our climate will be swarthy, probably very nearly that of the Spaniards who live in the same parallels. Are we then to be surprised that the African, who, under a tropical sun, bears the accumulated stain of a thousand generations, is not, in our climate, bleached white in two or three?'

Thus you see that reason and observation unite

in confirming the truth of revelation with regard to the color of the Africans. Hence we conclude with safety, that a black skin is no peculiar mark of Heaven's displeasure, nor any evidence that he who wears it is doomed by the Creator to endless servitude. The Africans are the children of our common mother: let us not be angry with them because the sun hath looked upon them; the change of complexion ought never to break the ties of humanity. God 'hath made of one blood all nations of men.' Whenever we find a man, let us treat him as a brother without regard to his color; let our kindness sooth his sorrows and cheer his heart.

II. The Africans are deeply degraded. The hand of oppression has pressed them down from the rank of men to that of beasts; they are bought and sold, and driven from place to place like mere animal herds;—this fetters the mind, and prevents that expansion of soul which dignifies man and ornaments civilized life. They seldom have any opportunities of improvement, any encouragement for the efforts of genius, or any inducements to enter the field of science. Hence, in many instances, the strongest powers of mind remain unfolded; over them oppression draws her sable mantle, on them she lays her cruel hand, and forbids them ever to rise. Under such circumstances they sink into the grossest ignorance, and appear to be very destitute of energetic powers of mind. This leads many to conclude that they are naturally inferior to the rest of mankind in respect to strength of mind, and that the Creator has thus marked them out for servitude. But how false, how ungenerous, how unreasonable is such a conclusion! What people, in similar circumstances, have ever given stronger marks of genius than are exhibited by the enslaved Africans in the United States? A better exhibition of mental capacity than they give ought not to be expected from a people long enslaved and sorely oppressed. Under such oppression, powers of mind, merely ordinary, cannot unfold; the gloomy prospect of perpetual bondage hovers continually around, and cuts off every enterprise which might elicit the native energies of the soul, or give occasion for the vigorous efforts of genius. Hence talents that, under other circumstances, would appear to very good advantage, are totally obscured. And, even after a people that have long been enslaved are emancipated, it will require them to pass through several generations in order to regain their original strength of mind, and give the world a fair exhibition of the powers they really possess. Under this view of our subject, it is easy to account for the apparent want of talent in our Africans; it is owing, totally owing, to the cruel hand of oppression. There is but one other source from which we suppose it will be pretended it has originated; which is that of a different organization from the rest of mankind. But such organization would be universal in its effects, and thus prohibit a single instance of prodigious genius; for if it admit of one, it may, on the same principles, admit of a thousand. Among the Africans there are many who possess the strongest powers of mind; this I apprehend none that are well informed will deny.

In a neighboring State lives an African boy, who, while he was a slave, and before he arrived to twenty years of age, by his own exertions, without the benefit of a school, save for the space of two weeks, acquired the science of reading, writing, arithmetic and geography, and made some advances in astronomy. Would Sir Isaac Newton have done more, had he been a slave?

While other slaves spent in idleness the few leisure moments allowed them, this youth was engaged in acquiring useful knowledge, and he had what is generally called a humane master, who, perhaps, gave him some instruction. Would not this youth, under other circumstances, have dazzled the eyes of the civilized world by the brilliant display of powerful intellect? Not the mountain weight of oppression could wholly suppress his gigantic power — in vain slavery with her sable mantle attempts to shroud his luminous mind — it breaks through the darkest shades — its noble energies rise beneath the ponderous mass, scan the power of numbers, grasp the circumference of the earth, and stretch a line to the stars. Such an instance of remarkable genius among the Africans, shows that the organization of their mental powers is equal to that of the rest of mankind. And how can it be otherwise, seeing all mankind originally sprang from one common parent, and consequently possess precisely the same nature?

III. In connection with the bias of mind which may arise against the Africans, in consequence of their color and degradation, I wish to mention another which is more powerful in its nature, and more injurious in its effects; it is that which arises from love of gain, and has a most blinding influence upon the mind; with thousands it is heavier than sand, while the strongest arguments are lighter than feathers. The love of gain is the polluted fountain whence issue all the dreadful evils that pervade our world; it gives energy to the tyrant's sword, it drenches the earth with blood, and binds whole nations in chains; from it every argument is drawn in favor of cruel injustice; it is the nauseous source of every hateful crime. The love of gain first introduced slavery into the world, and has been its constant support in every age. It was the love of gain that first enslaved the African race, and it now invents every possible argument against their emancipation. This is equally manifested in the social circle, and on the legislative floor; individuals and States will argue in favor of slavery in proportion as they view their interest at stake. And no doubt they often argue according to what they suppose to be right; though naturally honest as other men, they are pressed to the side of injustice by the weight of interest. And thus we often see the love of gain weighing down the finest feelings of the soul, blunting the most acute powers of perception, crushing the strongest faculty of judgment, breaking the most powerful ties of humanity, falling upon the unhappy African and binding him in chains of perpetual bondage! When once it takes full possession of the heart, the strongest faculties yield to its influence; it triumphs alike over the polished statesman, the courageous general, the accomplished gentleman, and the humble peasant. Its principal power lies in concealment; it operates under a thousand different masks; unperceived it obtrudes itself upon every order, it pervades the bar, finds its way to the hearts of judge and jury; it even enters the sanctuary and climbs the altar. The best of men are liable to yield too far to the love of gain, especially when large sacrifices must attend a right decision. And you, my dear brother, have considerable at stake; you must wade through much loss, if you would come to a right conclusion, and obey the imperious voice of justice; but remember that loss will be temporal, and from it may spring eternal gain. Therefore it is better to lose for the sake of doing justice, than to gain by oppression. Hence I entreat you let temporal interest have no influence upon your mind; divest yourself of every prejudice; throw open all the faculties of the soul for a fair and full investigation of the subject under consideration, and let an ardent desire to know the very truth be the governing principle; and you shall not wander long in the maze of error, nor stray far from the path of truth. Give me, I pray you, a candid ear while I plead with you for a poor, dejected and despised people, who dare not plead for themselves, and for whom, alas! too few will either lift the tongue or move a pen. Let not their color, their degradation, nor the predominating principle of self-interest, bias your mind against them. Let their miseries excite your pity, and incline you to justice.

In my next I will endeavor to prove from the nature of the Africans that they were not created for slavery. FROM YOUR BROTHER.

LETTER II.

LOVING BROTHER:

I hope, by this time, your mind is divested of every prejudice against the Africans, and that you have opened a candid ear to their plea for liberty. Inspired by this hope I now proceed, according to promise made in my last, to prove from the nature of the Africans that they were not created for slavery.

The Creator is infinitely wise, and consequently must have created every being in his universe for occupying some particular station in the scale of created existence. To suppose him to create without design, is to suppose him unwise. Again, if he has created every being to occupy a particular station in the scale of existence, he must have adapted the nature of every being to the station for which it was intended. To create for a particular purpose, and not adapt the thing created to that purpose, would argue the greatest want of wisdom. Hence we conclude that if the Creator formed the Africans for slavery, he has suited their nature to the design of their creation, and that they are incapacitated for freedom. This would be according to the whole analogy of creation, in which every creature has a nature suited to the station for which it was intended. But we find that the Africans are rational creatures, are of the human species, possess all the original properties of human nature, and consequently are capacitated for freedom; and such capacity shows the design of their creation. It is most absurd to imagine that beings created with capacity for liberty were designed for bondage. Did the capacity for freedom stand alone, it might itself be considered an argument sufficient to establish our point; but it stands not alone; it combines with it all the original properties of human nature; with it all these unite as so many heralds sent by the Almighty to declare that man never was formed for involuntary slavery. Every man, who possesses all the original properties of humanity, desires to obtain knowledge, wealth, reputation, liberty, and a vast variety of other objects which are necessary to complete his happiness. Now who does not see how inconsistent slavery is with the acquirement and enjoyment of all these objects of desire, and how directly it is opposed to the happiness of man? It obstructs the natural channels in which all his passions were designed to flow, contracts the whole sphere of mental operation, and offers violence to the strongest propensities of his nature. Does he desire to enter the delightful paths of science, and store his mind with such knowledge as is calculated to expand the noble powers of the soul, and raise man to the dignified station for which he was designed? This is forbidden; an indignant master frowns upon him, and drives him back into the shades of ignorance and hopeless toil. Does he wish to acquire such property as may be necessary to render him comfortable in his passage through life? Even this is denied him; he is doomed to labor all his days in heaping up treasure for another; and to death, fraught with terrors as it is, he must look for deliverance, and to the gloomy grave he must go as his only asylum from his sufferings and toils. Does he incline to move in the honorable and useful spheres of civil society? It is considered a crime for him to aspire above the rank of the grovelling beast: he must content himself with being bought and sold, and driven in chains from State to State, as a capricious avarice may dictate. Does he desire to enter the conjugal state, and partake of hymeneal enjoyment? The pleasure of any unfeeling master may forbid the object of his choice, and cause him to languish beneath the ravages of disappointed affection. Or is he a tender husband? He must see the object of his warmest affection bleeding beneath the torturing lash—her cries and her tears penetrate the inmost recesses of his heart, and seem ready to burst the tender fibres that twine around the seat of life; floods of tenderness roll from his eyes, but his sympathies cannot stay the cruel hand of the vengeful tyrant, nor heal the wounds inflicted by his malice. He dare not even attempt to console her grief by the language of tenderness, nor to wipe away her tears with the soft hand of compassion. I cannot conceive how flesh and blood can bear so much! You, brother, once sustained the relation of husband, and doubtless possessed all the tenderness of that endearing relation; and though the object of your warmest embraces now lies cold and silent in the grave, yet her very dust is dear to you, and her memory awakes the liveliest emotions in your heart; and how dreadful was the hour of final separation, when cruel death closed her youthful eyes, that beamed upon you with such innocence and love as banished the sorrows and cares of life! And how cruel was that shroud which inclosed from your sight the beauteous form that so often enraptured your heart! Tell me, dear brother, how could you have endured to see her tender frame bleed beneath the lacerating whip? Could you have witnessed her innocent tears and cries, without being overwhelmed with the mingled floods of compassion, resentment and grief? Little less near to you is the dear little daughter, and only child, whom you cherish with almost unequalled tenderness! How could you bear to see her tender skin cruelly torn by the torturing lash of a wicked master, whose heart by cruel indulgence has become totally estranged from the feelings of compassion? Would not such a scene shock the whole current of your nature, and turn all the streams of tenderness into the channel of direful revenge, which even the fear of a most terrible death could scarcely restrain? Slavery is often clothed with such scenes of cruelty and blood, and often sports with everything that is dear to man! — it breaks the most tender relations of life. Tell me not that the Africans are destitute of the fine feelings of tenderness towards their wives and children, which are manifested by the rest of mankind. The flood of grief that rolls over the sable and wo-worn cheek, when a wife or a child is snatched from the embraces of the fond husband or parent, speaks the passions of the soul in a language too strong to be resisted by anything less than implacable prejudice! Slavery interferes with all the social and relative duties, and what is still a more serious evil, it interferes with the divine prerogative over man, and robs the Almighty of the service which is due to him from the creatures of his power.

Finally, every man desires to be free, and this desire the Creator himself has implanted in the bosoms of all our race, and is certainly a conclusive proof that all were designed for freedom; else man was created for disappointment and misery. All the feelings of humanity are strongly opposed to being enslaved, and nothing but the strong arm of power can make man submit to the yoke of bondage. What, my brother, would be more distressing to you, than to have the yoke of slavery put upon your neck and that of your little daughter, that you might, with her, wear out your life in laboring for the wealth and ease of one who perhaps would not regard a single tender feeling of your nature? And though you think your slaves are in very comfortable circumstances, and I have no doubt but you treat them as kindly as is compatible with their present station, yet were you and your little daughter in the very same circumstances in which they are now placed, I think I would cheerfully part with all I possess to purchase your freedom, if nothing less would procure it; and if I should not, I apprehend you would think me an ungenerous and cruel brother. How then can you withhold from others what is so dear to yourself? The Africans possess all the original properties of humanity, and were, as we have fairly proven from their nature, created for freedom; and, therefore, to enslave them is both unjust and cruel.

In my next I intend to point out, more fully than I have done in this, some of the evils that attend slavery.

I AM YOURS IN FRATERNAL AFFECTION.

LETTER III.

MY DEAR BROTHER:

As involuntary slavery is opposed to all the original properties of human nature, it may be expected to involve its subjects in a vast variety of the most serious evils. And some of these, according to an intimation given in my last, I am now to point out more fully than the limits of the preceding letter would permit me to do. And this I do in order to illustrate and enforce those arguments against slavery, which arise from the nature of man.

The first evil I shall mention as resulting from a state of mancipation, is that of gross ignorance. It must be obvious to every one capable of reflection, that a variety of circumstances combine to deprive slaves of the means of mental improvement. They are chained down to a life of laborious servitude, without the hope of release; and the gloomy prospect of such a life sinks every rising hope, cuts off every inducement to literary enterprise, and totally indisposes the mind to the labor of acquiring useful knowledge. And of such indisposition, gross ignorance is the certain result. Hence were the means of instruction afforded them, they would in many cases prove entirely unsuccessful. But we often find on the part of the master still less inclination to afford such means, than there is in the slave to improve them when afforded. The education of slaves must be attended with much loss of labor as well as considerable expense, and this is very inconsistent with the main object of their mancipation. The design of slaveholding is to make gain, and therefore few masters are willing to undergo the expense and loss of time from labor that must necessarily attend the education of their slaves. And this is no matter of wonder, when many parents are too avaricious to bear the expense of educating their own children. Now when parental affection is often insufficient to break the fetters of avarice, and induce parents to afford their own offspring the ample means of mental improvement, what can break loose the ice-bound heart of the man who is urged by the impetuous torrent of avaricious feeling to bind with the chains of mancipation a number of his fellow-creatures, and cause them, hungry and naked, to toil throughout life in heaping up treasure to satisfy his inordinate and rapidly increasing thirst for gain? I say, what can break loose the heart of such a man, inspire him with the feelings of tenderness towards the victims of his avarice, and induce him to sacrifice his gain in giving them that knowledge which is unnecessary to fit them for the laborious task? To this nothing can induce him while the love of gain is the predominating principle, and such, doubtless, will be the case while slavery exists in the world; for the very moment the principle of justice gains the ascendancy over that of avarice, must slavery cease to exist. Avarice tends to enslave, but justice requires emancipation. And nothing can be more evident than that the very principle in which slavery originates, withholds from the enslaved the means of acquiring knowledge, and consequently ignorance must be the necessary result. And to this we may add, that when the slave population becomes extensive, a carnal policy dictates the necessity of suppressing the means of information, lest the oppressed should come to know their rights, and endanger the state. This kind of policy prevails to such a degree in every slaveholding State, that there are very few places in which there is not strong opposition made to every benevolent attempt to teach the poor slaves to read even the words of eternal life! I know from experience that this is the case, even where slavery exists under its best and mildest form. Thus I believe it does exist in the State of Kentucky. If there be any place in the United States where it wears a tolerable aspect, I am persuaded it is in that State; and though, as you know, I am no Kentuckian, yet I must say that if any slaveholding people can be generous, the Kentuckians are such. But the mildest form of slavery is like 'the tender mercies of the wicked,' very cruel. Though there is no law in Kentucky designed to prohibit the teaching of slaves, yet such is the opposition made against it by the populace, that but few Sabbath-schools for the instruction of the Africans are permitted to exist in the State. It often happens that the benevolent teachers of Sabbath-schools find themselves, and their poor, unoffending scholars, on the sacred morning, surrounded by men armed with whips, clubs and guns, for the violent dispersion of the unhappy and innocent victims of their rage! Thus Sabbath-schools are broken up in Kentucky with a violence and cruelty that ought to shame the most unfeeling band of Algerines! Nor is such violent opposition to teaching slaves confined to the more ignorant parts of the State; it is equally manifested in the most enlightened places. A few years since in the neighborhood of Lexington, and in one of the oldest and best settlements in the State, a Sabbath-school was instituted, and taught by some very respectable gentlemen, and the prospect of doing good was exceedingly fair; but, alas! all the rising hopes of benevolence were soon blasted. One sacred morning the poor slaves assembled at the school-room with the pleasing expectation of learning to read the word of eternal life; but to their sad surprise, about sixty men soon appeared for their dispersion, armed with clubs and guns, and thus the school was dispersed never to meet again! It is painful to record such instances of cruel outrage on oppressed innocence and humane feeling; and I do it not by way of reproach, but because it is necessary to show the real state of things even where slavery assumes her mildest aspect; for I still believe that slaves fare upon the whole better in Kentucky than they do in other slaveholding States. But the spirit which, in Kentucky, is so strongly manifested by the populace, has, it seems, in Virginia found its way into the Legislature.* And, as I am in-

* Extract from a letter to the Editor of the Emancipator, from a correspondent in Norfolk, Virginia, dated

AUGUST, 27, 1831.

There is now a law in this State, which took place on the 1st day of January last, which prohibits schools being kept for teaching colored people, under the penalty of three dollars for every offence, if free, or twenty lashes on the bare back; or if slaves, twenty lashes. It subjects white persons to the same penalty; and enjoins on all magistrates and sheriffs, under the penalty of eight dollars for refusing, to execute the law. The informer is to have the whole of the fine

My wife, who had a Sabbath-school for colored children, which she taught gratis for three or four years past, has been compelled to give it up, although none were admitted but those who were free, and those who had written permits from their owners. She had more than one hundred scholars at a time; and although the school was supported by some of the best men in town, and several of the magistrates, yet I was presented before the grand jury, and nothing saved me but the presentment being made

formed, a law has, sometime since, actually passed, prohibiting all, and every person from teaching a school for the benefit of slaves, under the penalty of twenty lashes! And thus the last hope of the poor, oppressed African is cut off—the clouds of ignorance, like the shades of eternal night, must ever settle around him! And thus the innocent and good citizen, whose feeling stoops to the most oppressed and degraded of our race, in order to grasp them from interminable ruin, must be subjected to the painful and shameful penalty of twenty lashes, as the reward of most disinterested acts of kindness, and that in a land far-famed for the equity and mildness of its government! Oh! tell it not in Europe, publish it not in the courts of despotism, lest the European despots rejoice! Thus has Virginia disgraced her nation, she has shrouded the rising glories of the American government, and she now hangs, as a ponderous mass, upon the wing of the American eagle, and prevents her from soaring to the sublime heights of pure republican liberty! Instead of removing every vestige of oppression, she is strengthening the yoke and tightening the chains of cruel bondage! This violent opposition to the instruction of slaves, whether it arises from a mistaken policy or from avaricious motives, will increase in proportion as the slave population becomes more extensive. And here I must remark upon one main objection to the emancipation of slaves; it is that they are, in consequence of the want of information, incapacitated for freedom,

before the law became in force. Before I consented for the school to be broke up, I consulted with the State's attorney, who was much in favor of the school, and a pious man, who said that it was so pointedly against the law, that he himself as the prosecutor, would be obliged to take notice of it.

I am so disgusted with my native State, that if I could dispose of my property without too great sacrifice, old as I am, I would remove to a land of liberty!

and that it is necessary to detain them in bondage until they may be better prepared for liberation; but from the preceding remarks it is abundantly evident that they are now better prepared, with respect to information, for emancipation, than they will be at any future period, and that less inconvenience and danger would attend their liberation at the present than at any future time. It must be obvious to every one capable of discernment, that the inconvenience and danger of emancipation will increase in proportion as slaves become more numerous. Indeed all the difficulties that attend emancipation are rapidly increasing; and they must certainly be endured at some period, sooner or later; for it is most absurd to imagine that such an immense body of people, most rapidly increasing, can always be retained in bondage; and therefore it is much better to endure those difficulties now than it will be when they shall have grown to the most enormous size. But perhaps you may hope that the benign influence of the gospel will remove the obstacles that now lie in the way of teaching slaves, and consequently will lessen the difficulties that now attend their liberation; and that such would be the tendency of the gospel, were its influence generally and truly felt, I readily admit; but this cannot be reasonably expected, when we consider that a vast variety of obstacles combine to prevent the prevalence of evangelical feeling in slaveholding States. The whole system of slavery is unfavorable, in its consequences as well as in its nature, to the extension of gospel influence. I readily acknowledge that there are, in all the slaveholding States, some who possess so high a degree of moral feeling as induces them, amidst sneering opposition, to pay some conscientious regard to the religious education of their slaves; but such are very rarely found, even among those who profess Christianity, and much less must be expected from the unbelieving world. It is a matter of deep regret, that a large number of those who profess to be Christians, have not religion enough to induce them to give proper attention to the education of their own offspring, and certainly such will pay much less attention to the education of slaves. It is undeniable, that many of the slaveholding clergy and ruling elders do not teach their slaves to read the scriptures, nor even cause them to attend upon their family devotion! I have seen the preacher and elder bow their knees around the family altar, while their poor slaves remained without, as if, like mere animal herds, they had no interest in the morning and evening sacrifices! Now when men who profess to believe and teach the mild and benevolent principles of the gospel, can be so destitute of evangelical feeling as totally to neglect the instruction of their slaves, what must be expected from those who scorn the sacred volume, and regard none of its heavenly precepts? Hence I must still conclude that gross ignorance in the enslaved must be the certain result of involuntary slavery, even where it assumes its mildest forms.

My letter is, perhaps, already too long, and therefore I must desist for the present. You may expect me to pursue the subject in my next.

FAREWELL, MY BROTHER.

LETTER IV.

LOVING BROTHER:

The slave population in every country where slavery exists, is in a state of gross ignorance, and this confirms the arguments adduced, in the preceding letter, to show that such ignorance must be the certain result of involuntary slavery, even where it wears the mildest aspect. And that this is a very serious evil will appear, if we duly consider its tendency. And to this design, at present, I invite your attention.

I have already shown, in a preceding letter, that many of the Africans possess the finest powers of mind, and that, in this respect, they are naturally equal to the rest of mankind. Now take a view of the slave population in the United States, and you will see that a vast quantity of the very best talent is entirely suppressed by want of suitable means of improvement — it lies buried deeply in the wreck of liberty, and the cruel hand of oppression draws around it the dark shades of endless night. Thus brilliant talents, immortal powers, designed to enrich, illuminate and aggrandize the world, lie dormant and useless beneath the grossest covering of unavoidable ignorance! and all that is noble and grand in our nature, wastes in the drudgery of a servile life! Were all the talent that is now suppressed by slavery, in all our slaveholding States, properly improved, liberated, and brought into action, how vastly would it add to the strength, wealth, and intelligence of our nation! There are at present, in different parts of our country, a considerable number of amiable and wealthy inhabitants, who were once in a state of bondage.

The Rev. John Gloucester, lately pastor of an African church in the city of Philadelphia, but now no more in time, passed a considerable part of his life in slavery, yet after his liberation he became an able and useful minister of the gospel. His piety and talents recommended him to the benevolence of Union Presbytery, East Tennessee, by whose generous exertions he, with his wife and children, were liberated from bondage; and he educated, and afterwards set apart to the gospel ministry. And though he spent in servitude the part of life in which the powers of the mind are most susceptible of improvement, yet the strength of his mind was such as enabled him soon to acquire so considerable a fund of knowledge as rendered him an useful and acceptable preacher, both to the white and black inhabitants of Philadelphia. He possessed, as we believe, the confidence and esteem of his brethren in the ministry, some of whom are among the most eminent in our nation for piety, talents and literature. Had it not been for the benevolence of Union Presbytery, this man, amiable as he was, in the possession of the strongest powers of mind, and all the fine sensibilities of our nature ornamented and improved by the renovating influence of divine grace, must have worn throughout life the iron yoke of cruel and unjust bondage! He is now released from all his labors and sufferings; and though here he was covered with a sable skin, and was once a poor, dejected and despised slave, we have reason to believe he will shine forever as a bright star in the firmament of eternal glory! Who would not execrate the chains that bound such a man! And such the chains of slavery did bind, and thousands such they do still bind, and cause to wear out their lives in degradation and misery! Thus the finest powers of soul which the benevolent Creator has bestowed on man and designed for the noblest exercise and the noblest ends, are defaced and deprived of the means of useful operation, and consequently are entirely lost to the world! Such suppression of useful talent is certainly a sore evil.

Union Presbytery has been the means of liberating and educating another man of color, who is now preaching the gospel. And though he was far advanced in life before his liberation, yet he, in preaching, excels many white men who in early life have had all the advantages of a liberal education! I have myself heard him deliver some discourses that would be no discredit to the best of talents in a state of the best improvement! Thus Union Presbytery has given the world to see what vast improvement poor African slaves are capable of making, even after spending the prime of life in oppressive servitude!

It is with pleasure I speak of the benevolence of that Presbytery, because they have opposed slavery, not in word only, but also in deed. They have done much to wipe away the reproach of the hapless and degraded Africans, and have shown, by actual experiment, that they are capable of the highest degree of mental improvement, and of filling the most useful stations in the civilized world. How much good might other Presbyteries, Conferences and Associations do, by copying their example !

Again, the ignorance which results from slavery is a fruitful source of immorality, and consequently a very serious evil.

Such is the corrupt tendency of human nature that nothing short of a high degree of moral sensation is sufficient to restrain man from vicious indulgence. And to such sensation knowledge is indispensably necessary. The cannibal kills and eats a man with as little consciousness of guilt as a Christian feels when he slaughters and eats his animal herds, and yet rational powers are alike common to both ; but the one is involved in the grossest ignorance, while the other possesses a knowledge of the purest standard of moral rectitude. Hence the one is estranged from moral feeling while the other possesses it to a high degree, and consequently is shocked at the very idea of killing and eating his fellow man! The poor African slaves are generally raised without moral instruction, and therefore are but little acquainted with the character of God, the purity of his law, their obligations to obey it, and the happiness that springs from piety, or the miseries that arise from vice; and consequently they possess a very low degree of moral feeling; and this renders them an easy prey to the corrupt propensities of their nature. And in addition to this, they are deprived of such motives to virtuous conduct as arise from reputation and honor. Thus everything that was calculated to stem the impetuous torrent of vicious feeling and inspire them with the love of virtue, is taken from them. Hence, regardless of all consequences, they rush into the deepest abyss of the most destructive and degrading immorality! Their being slaves to men becomes the principal means of making them slaves to vice. And this evil assumes a still more dreadful aspect when it is viewed in connection with eternity. It is not only a deep source of misery in time, but it is also a never-failing fountain of suffering in the world to come; it incapacitates the soul for celestial enjoyment, and prepares it for the doleful abodes of endless wo. Oh! hapless immortals! Their sufferings here are but the beginnings of endless sorrows! They are too deeply sunk in pollution to enter, as they are, into the pure abodes of bliss; and cruel oppression forbids them to bathe in the fountain of life, to wash away their guilt, and fit them for the heavenly state! The key of knowledge is taken away, the path of life is closed up, and the immortal mind is sealed in everlasting night! 'Where there is no vision the people perish.' And, alas!

millions of poor disconsolate slaves have no vision —the lamp of life is not permitted to illuminate their dreary huts or cheer their wo-worn hearts with the soul enlivening beams of heavenly light! Thick moral darkness, without interruption, dwells in all their abodes, and the shades of endless despair settle around them — they have nothing in time but the prospect of misery and toil, and nothing beyond but the prospect of interminable wo! Thus slavery chains men down to a life of labor and sufferings in this word, and by depriving them of the means of salvation, chains them down to everlasting misery in the world to come! And thousands of the most worthless of our race are not only rioting on the wreck of liberty, but actually rioting on the wreck of the immortal mind — the very bread they eat is died in the blood of souls! 'O my soul, come not thou into their secret; unto their assembly, mine honor, be not thou united;' for their tyranny is more terrible than death, and their avarice more cruel than the grave!

You tell me that many of the poor Africans will be thankful that they were brought from the dark regions of Africa, and made slaves in a land of gospel-light, where they have become the subjects of salvation! And on this ground many justify themselves in holding slaves, and on the same principle the Jews might have justified themselves in crucifying the Saviour; for by it redemption was brought to a ruined world; but we ought to remember that it is the province of the Almighty to bring good out of evil, and that it is not the province of man to 'Do evil that good may come.' We have no right to promote the curse of slavery because a benevolent Providence sometimes turns it into a blessing. The question with us is not whether the Africans are now in a better or worse condition than they would have been in their own country; but this is the question — is it just for us to enslave them, and by it render them miserable in life, and deprive them of the means of happiness beyond the grave? It is undeniable that their being slaves to men involves them in ignorance, and makes them slaves of vice, and so becomes a source of endless misery.

Let me now in the close of this letter invite you to call up all the tender sensibilities of your nature, and drop a tear of compassion over the vast multitudes of hapless Africans who are marching on to eternity fast-bound in the fetters of ignorance and vice — pursue them to the grave, pursue them beyond it, and see what dreadful misery entails on our fellow immortals! And while your sympathies are aroused, remember that you have practically sanctioned slavery, which is the source of their terrible sufferings, and that it is not all your kindness to your slaves can atone for such a crime! Remember, you must 'Do justly, love mercy — break every yoke, and let the oppressed go free.'

LETTER V.

DEAR BROTHER:

The longer I reflect upon involuntary slavery, the more I abhor it, as being a combination of the most flagrant injustice and cruelty. It makes an innocent man the property of another, who may, if he please, deprive him of all the comforts of life, and subject him to a thousand sufferings. This appears to me as most unjust and cruel, when

I consider that the very best of men are fallen creatures, and, as such, naturally disposed to tyrannize over the subjects of their power. The history of the world is but one general display of tyrannical oppression — every nation has been made to agonize beneath the weight of cruel despotism; every sect or party, that has in any age been vested with absolute power, whether civil or ecclesiastical, has manifested a strong tendency towards tyranny. Indeed such corrupt tendency marks the whole character of a fallen man, and is often displayed where the God of nature seems to have placed the strongest guard against it — parents frequently break over the strong barrier of natural affection, and oppress their own offspring. It is true that some men are more humane than others, yet even such are liable to tyrannize, in some instances, over the subjects of their power. Hence David, though one of the most humane princes of antiquity, exercised most horrible tyranny in the case of Uriah ; and the personal attendants of the Saviour, though they had heard from his sacred lips the most tender lessons of compassion, were anxious to command fire down from Heaven, in order to consume a whole city! Thus we see how the corruptions of the very best of men occasionally triumph over them, and, with dreadful impetuosity hurry them into scenes of most shocking cruelty ! Hence we conclude that the very best of men are disqualified for the proper exercise of such absolute power as involuntary slavery confers on the proprietor of slaves. And how much less the worst of men are qualified for the suitable exercise of such power, will appear more evidently, while we consider the immense degree to which it extends.

I. The law of involuntary slavery makes the slave the property of his master, who is no more bound to supply his natural wants, than he is to supply those of his beasts. But notwithstanding the slave is shoved down to the rank of the beast, he is still a man, and needs comfortable clothing to shield him from the chilling blasts of winter, as well as for the sake of decent appearance. And this the master is not bound to give him, but may either clothe him in rags or turn him naked, as an inordinate love of gain may dictate. Hence in some parts of Alabama you may see slaves in the cotton-fields without so much as even a single rag upon them, shivering before the chilling blasts of mid-winter. In some sections of old Virginia, they have been seen naked as in the hour of their birth attending on their master's table. And doubtless the like may be seen in South Carolina, Georgia and Mississippi. Indeed in every slaveholding state many slaves suffer extremely, both while they labor and while they sleep, for want of clothing to keep them warm. Often they are driven through frost and snow without either stocking or shoe, until the path they tread is dyed with the blood that issues from their frost-worn limbs! And when they return to their miserable huts at night they find not there the means of comfortable rest; but on the cold ground they must lie without covering, and shiver while they slumber.

In connection with their extreme sufferings occasioned by want of clothing I shall notice those which arise from the want of food. As the making of grain is the main object of their mancipation, masters will sacrifice as little as possible in giving them food. It often happens that what will barely keep them alive, is all that a cruel avarice will allow them. Hence, in some instances, their allowance has been reduced to a single pint of corn each during the day and night. And some have no better allowance than a small portion of cotton seed ! ! And in some places the best allowance is a peck of corn each during the week, while perhaps they are not permitted to taste meat so much as once in the course of seven years, except what little they may be able to steal ! Thousands of them are pressed with the gnawings of cruel hunger during their whole lives ; an insatiable avarice will not grant them a single comfortable meal to satisfy the cravings of nature ! Such cruelty far exceeds the powers of description.*

You tell me that 'If the poor negroes were set free, they would either starve or turn to highway robbing.' But certainly their situation could not be worse than it now is with regard to starvation and robbing. Thousands of them are really starving in a state of slavery, and are under the direful necessity of stealing whatever they can find that will satisfy the cravings of hunger ; and I have little doubt but many actually starve to death. Should they starve when free, the fault would, in some measure, be their own; and should they steal they could be punished for it in the same manner that white thieves are punished for their thefts.

II. The slaveholder has it in his power to violate the chastity of his slaves. And not a few are beastly enough to exercise such power. Hence it happens that, in some families, it is difficult to distinguish the free children from the slaves. It

* Alas, poor hapless slaves are doomed to toil,
With naked limbs, beneath the direful rage
Of fiercely burning suns, and chilling blasts
That beat upon them with alternate strokes ;
While long years of fierce starvation onward
Roll, with lingering pace, and the grating wheels
Of time, that measure out the dreary span
Of hard servile life scarcely seem to move,
And the toil-worn and weather-beaten flesh,
Longs for the peaceful, lasting sleep of death,
And seeks a shelter in the silent grave,
From hunger, toil, and raging elements.

is sometimes the case that the largest part of the master's own children, are born, not of his wife, but of the wives and daughters of his slaves, whom he has basely prostituted as well as enslaved. His poor slaves are his property, and therefore must yield to his lusts as well as to his avarice! He may perpetrate upon them the most horrid crimes, and they have no redress! The wretched slave must, without a murmuring word, give up his wife or daughter for prostitution, should his master be vile enough to demand her of him! It must be a horrid crime for any State to give one man such power over another; and such crime has every slaveholding State committed. I am far from wishing to intimate that this power is generally so grossly exercised as it might be. Some slaveholders are, doubtless, as chaste as any other people, and conscientiously endeavor to preserve the chastity of their slaves; but I wish to show the extent of the power with which they are vested, and the shocking manner in which it is sometimes exercised.

In addition to this, we may remark, that the proprietors of slaves have it in their power to crowd the males and females together in such a manner as is calculated to induce criminal intercourse, and to the great disgrace of human nature this is sometimes done for the base purpose of breeding slaves for market, as though they were mere animals and not human beings!

In this place I will further remark, that slavery not merely puts the chastity of the slave in the power of the master, but also exposes it to attacks from every lecherous class of men. Slaves cannot bear testimony against people that are white and free — hence a wide door is opened for the practice, both of violence and seduction, without detection; and the consequences of this are exceedingly manifested in every slaveholding country — every town and its vicinity soon become crowded with mulattoes. In this respect slavery is the very sink of filthiness, and the source of every hateful abomination. It seems to me astonishing that any government, much more that of the United States, should sanction such a source of monstrous crime as slavery evidently is! And I am still more astonished that you, my brother, should countenance it in the least degree, either in theory or practice. It is fraught with such horrible abominations as ought to shock you and cause you to shrink from its first approaches. I would rather beg my bread from door to door, long as I live, than enslave even the meanest of my fellow creatures. My soul abhors the crime.

I intend to dwell more upon the horrors of slavery in my next. FAREWELL BROTHER.

LETTER VI.

AFFECTIONATE BROTHER:

In the preceding letter I commenced pointing out the extent of the slaveholder's power over his slaves, and therefore, in the present, I intend to continue the course thus begun.

I have already shown that the proprietors of slaves may deprive them of food and raiment, and even violate their chastity as well as place them in such circumstances as are unfavorable to purity.

And did their power extend no further than these particulars, it would in other respects be well for poor slaves; but alas, these are merely the beginnings of their miseries! And therefore in connection with the remarks made in the preceding letter, I further observe that the slaveholder's power extends over the married relation among his slaves. He may prohibit them from forming that relation, and may also violate it after it is formed, and the exercise of such power often becomes a source of great misery.

One of the most imperious laws of human nature is, that a man shall leave his father and his mother and cleave unto his wife. 'And the two shall be one flesh.' Mutual affection between the parties is the foundation upon which the married relation ought to be formed, and it is also the principal source of happiness after its formation. Hence the voices of nature and revelation unite in declaring that every man who has come to mature age, ought to have liberty to possess the person of his choice when it is reciprocated by the person chosen. But a domineering master may prohibit his slave from enjoying the object of his choice, and doom him either to choose perpetual celibacy, or to enter into the nuptial relation with a person on whom he cannot place his affections; and such alternative must be attended with most injurious effects. Perpetual celibacy, though not in every instance to be considered criminal, is evidently opposed to one of the strongest currents of nature, and one which sometimes, by unnatural obstruction, inundates the whole man, and involves him in dreadful ruin. And to marry a person for whom there is no affection, is to enter on a life of unabating misery — it opens a door to such domestic broils as nothing but final separation can terminate — it often becomes the means of the basest lewdness, and thus produces incalculable evil. We may reasonably conclude that much of the want of chastity which manifestly exists among slaves, has originated in the unjust control of their affections.

Again, the proprietors of slaves have power not merely to prohibit them from marrying the persons of their choice, but may even separate them from such after the nuptial relation is formed. Indeed slavery seems to be almost entirely incompatible with the married state. Slaves, like other property, are liable to be taken by execution and sold for debt, and so must fall into the hands of the highest bidders, who may drive them to some distant section of the country, and separate them from those to whom they are bound by the endearing relation of marriage. And they are liable to similar separation by falling into the hands of heirs who may scatter them abroad into far distant places. And we may further remark, that many wilfully sell their married slaves to men who follow the horrible practice of driving them to distant markets, without paying the least regard to any of the tender relations of life ! Hence it often happens that the poor slave, while laboring in the field, is suddenly seized by the cruel slavedriver, bound fast in iron fetters, and hurried off to a far distant market, without being permitted to return to his hapless hut, and there pour out his bursting floods of sorrow in taking his final leave of his disconsolate wife and children ! ! Had he ten thousand worlds he would gladly give them all for the warm embraces of his affectionate wife and fondling babes ! Oh ! what would he not give for the privilege of bathing the object of his affection in his parting tears ! The inmost recesses of his nature ardently crave the mingled floods of final separation ! ! But alas ! he must see the objects of his love no more! no more enjoy the warm embrace ! and no more must he clasp to his tender heart his prattling babes ! Hopeless man! witness the anguish of his heart! see what torrents gush from his eyes! behold his downcast and sorrowful aspect! listen to his plaintive sighs! hear his piteous cries and agonizing groans! His trembling nature racked in every part by the rising billows of sudden and overwhelming grief, calls for pity in accents melting as the doleful notes of expiring life! But all is in vain! The cruel slavedriver, long accustomed to such scenes of sorrow, remains unmoved by the agonizing groans of suffering humanity; he is so far estranged from every tender feeling, that he even sports himself with the sufferings of his fellow creatures; the groans of the poor slave seem to be as music to his ears, and the blood elicited by his torturing lash appears to be delightful to his eyes! In vain the bereaved husband, with languishing eye, looks for pity — the cruel whip urges him on to a far distant land — away he must move, loaded with weighty fetters, which are but faint emblems of his still more weighty sorrows — his affections linger far behind — his mind wanders far back, and hovers round the now disconsolate hut, where once the kind attentions of an affectionate wife and the innocent prattling of his sportive babes dispelled the gloom and sweetened the toils of a servile life. O could he now awake and find that all has been a frightful dream, how would his sorrowful heart rejoice! but, alas! all is dreadful reality. The last hope is gone! All that could cheer the heart and bear up the desponding mind amidst the sufferings and toils of unjust and cruel bondage, is gone! forever gone! horrible tyrants have robbed him of the last drop of consolation! His wife and children, unconscious of what has happened, long and anxiously wait his return; but, ah! he is never to return! never again to cheer the dreary hut with his presence, or gladden the hearts of his wife and children by his visits of love! His innocent hands are bound with cruel fetters, and wicked monsters are dragging him to a far distant land where he must throughout life endure still harder bondage, and even that embittered by the loss of all that is dear to an affectionate father and tender husband. At length the sad news arrives at the miserable hut that the father and husband is gone! gone in chains! gone to a distant land! gone to return no more! gone, not down to the peaceful chambers of death no more to weep, no more to sigh; but gone to a land where slavery sits upon her ebon throne, and thence dispenses all her blackest horrors! a land where starvation reigns in all its meagre forms! and where cruelty deals out long years of death! Hapless mother! hapless children! By relentless tyranny bereaved of every hope, of all that is dear on earth, and doomed to linger out a servile life in hopeless grief! The little hut is filled with throbs, and sighs, and agonizing groans! It is now more like the abodes of ruined spirits, in which doleful despair in midnight horror reigns, than like the abodes of man!

In the public papers of slaveholding States, you may see fathers and mothers, and husbands and wives, and children advertised for public sale, and that in connection with a variety of beasts. And in those States, while droves of slaves are collecting for a distant market, the public prisons are frequently crowded with parents and children, and husbands and wives, who are thus imprisoned for no other crime than that of loving their corresponding relatives! And as soon as the drove is completed, they are loaded with chains, and driven like beasts to a distant market! Thus in the boasted land of freedom you may hear the clanking chains of the most horrible oppression! Yes, in America, the far-famed America, you may hear the clankings of the chains that bind innocent husbands and wives, and parents and children, in order that they may be forever separated from the objects of their affections and all that is dear to them in life! Could the tyrannical Pharaoh be more cruel than are the slaveholding States?

These horrible things happen not merely where slavery assumes its worst form, but very frequently take place where it wears the mildest aspect: they often happen, even in Kentucky; and some years since a respectable petition praying for the prohibition of slave driving and its attendant cruelties, was forwarded to the Legislature, by a considerable number of the most humane citizens of that State, but was rejected! And thus Kentucky has, by the voice of her Legislature, said that she will not prohibit one of the most shocking cruelties ever inflicted on man. She has said she will not regard the tears and groans and dreadful sufferings of the poor and despised Africans. She has sanctioned all the horrors of slave-driving, and she, as a State, must answer for violating the most sacred rights of man.

Since the rejection of this humane petition, one of the grossest insults has in that State been offered to the general government of the United States, as well as to the most tender feelings of humanity, by the slavedriving Stone and Kinningham, of Bourbon Co., Kentucky. These unfeeling wretches purchased a considerable drove of slaves — how many of them were separated from husbands and wives, I will not pretend to say — and having chained a number of them together, hoisted over them the flag of American liberty, and with the music of two violins marched the wo-worn, heart-broken and sobbing creatures through the town of Paris!* Thus, in horrible contempt of the American government, innocent men are led in chains beneath its flag. And the eyes of the sublimely soaring eagle of American liberty are highly insulted while she is made to

* In relation to this matter I will give you the statements of the Rev. James H. Dickey, who met the drove to which I allude before it entered Paris.

"In the summer of 1822, as I returned with my family from a visit to the Barrens of Kentucky, I witnessed a scene such as I never witnessed before, and such as I hope never to witness again. Having passed through Paris, in Bourbon county, Ky., the sound of music (beyond a little rising ground) attracted my attention; I looked forward and saw the flag of my country waving. Supposing that I was about to meet a military parade, I drove hastily to the side of the road; and having gained the top of the ascent, I discovered (I suppose) about forty black men all chained together after the following manner; each of them was handcuffed, and they were arranged in rank and file. A chain, perhaps 40 feet long, the size of a fifth-horse-chain, was stretched between the two ranks, to which short chains were joined, which connected with the handcuffs. Behind them were, I suppose, about thirty women, in double rank, the couples tied hand to hand. A solemn sadness sat on every countenance, and the dismal silence of this march of despair was interrupted only by the sound of two violins; yes, as if to add insult to injury, the foremost couple were furnished with a violin apiece; the second couple were ornamented with cockades, while near the centre waved the Republican flag carried by a hand *literally in chains*. I perhaps have mistaken some punctilos of the arrangement, for 'my soul was sick,' my feelings were mingled and pungent. As a man, I sympathized with suffering humanity, as a Christian, I mourned over the transgressions of God's holy law, and as a *republican* I felt indignant, to see the flag of my beloved country thus insulted. I could not forbear exclaiming to the lordly driver who rode at his ease along side, 'Heaven will curse that man who engages in such traffic, and the government that protects him in it.' I pursued my journey till evening, and put up for the night; when I mentioned the scene I had witnessed, 'Ah!' cried my landlady, 'that is my brother.' From her I learned that his name is Stone, of Bourbon county, Kentucky, in partnership with one Kinningham of Paris; and that a few days before he had purchased a negro woman from a man in Nicholas county; she refused to go with him; he attempted to compel her, but she defended herself. Without farther ceremony, he stepped back and by a blow on the side of her head with the butt of his whip brought her to the ground; he tied her and drove her off. I learned farther, that besides the drove I had seen, there were about thirty shut up in the Paris prison for safe keeping, to be added to the company, and that they were destined for the Orleans market. And to this they are doomed for no other crime than that of a black skin and curled locks.

> Ah me, what wish can prosper, or what prayer
> For merchants rich in cargoes of despair!
> Who drive a loathsome traffic, guage and span,
> And buy the muscles and the bones of man. COWPER.

Shall I not visit for these things, saith the *Lord?* shall not my soul be avenged on such a nation as this!

But I forbear, and subscribe myself yours,

JAMES H. DICKEY.

September 30, 1824."

hover over the detestable chains of cruel bondage! And the feelings of humanity are shocked at seeing the most oppressive sorrows of suffering innocence mocked with all the lightness of sportive music! And who can help feeling indignant at seeing the American flag becoming the derision of tyrants!

O that every tender heart could be made acquainted with the sorrows of the poor enslaved Africans! O that every sympathetic ear could hear their agonizing groans. Then would the energies of our nation arise and demand their relief. But their sufferings are unknown; they far transcend the highest description that can be given by the pens of mortals!

Eternal Sovereign of the sky,
Wilt thou not hear the negro's sigh?
Wilt thou not break his galling chains,
And ease him from his dreadful pains?
Yes, mancipators all must feel
Thy vengeance like a racking wheel,
That on them shall forever turn,
Long as thy ceaseless wrath shall burn!

Beware, brother, lest this vengeance may light on you.

Perhaps you are tired of hearing of the horrors of slavery, but I feel disposed to dwell longer upon them. ADIEU FOR THE PRESENT.

LETTER VII.

AFFECTIONATE BROTHER:

I must still continue to unfold the extent of the slaveholder's power over his slaves.

In addition to what we have already said upon this subject, we remark that slaves are moral agents, and therefore are accountable creatures, and bound to worship God according to the dictates of his word; but a wicked master may actually prohibit them from obeying the ordinances of God, deprive them of hearing the gospel, and even compel them to do what is absolutely forbidden by the divine law, and what is entirely contrary to the dictates of their own consciences. And thus he is permitted to tyrannize over the consciences of men, which is the worst of all tyranny. The rights of conscience have, by all good men in every age of the world, been deemed most sacred. For them thousands of our ancestors beyond the great water shed the last drop of their blood, and for them thousands more fled to the savage wilderness of America, and have here erected the standard of religious liberty. 'They have made the solitary places glad, and the wilderness to blossom as the rose.' But in this now highly favored land, thousands of innocent men are enslaved, and deprived of the rights of conscience. They are, in many instances, prohibited from attending either to the concerns of their own souls, or those of their children. And nothing but some extraordinary exercise of divine sovereignty can prevent the wicked slaveholder from fixing the eternal destiny of his slaves. To give fallen men such absolute control over the eternal destinies of the immortal mind is cruel beyond all description. You perhaps may reply, that parents exercise a similar control over the destinies of their children, and that expressly by divine permission. To this I answer that the absolute power of parents over their children is sweetly tempered with parental affection, and is thus strongly guarded against injurious effects; and it extends no further than minor age, and they are solemnly commanded to use it with lenity, and to bring up their 'children in the nurture and admonition of the Lord.' Hence it is evident that the power of slaveholders over their slaves, and that of parents over their children, are essentially different ; the one is mild, natural and necessary, and the other is unnatural, unnecessary and cruel.

Again, the proprietors of slaves may exact from them excessive labor, and thus lay upon them an intolerable burden during life. It is well known that many masters are so avaricious that they cannot be satisfied with a reasonable quantity of labor. The manner in which these unfeeling monsters exact labor from their poor slaves may be illustrated by a single fact, the knowledge of which came to me from a respectable source, and though it appears most shocking to every humane feeling, yet I believe it can be fully attested.

A wealthy citizen of Georgia purchased, on shipboard, six African girls, who probably were directly from Africa, and having brought them home, he put them into the hands of his overseer, and ordered him to assign them a certain portion of labor during each day of the week, and in case they should fail to perform it, he was commanded to give them a considerable number of lashes each, and to add the remainder of the task to the next day's labor ; and in case they should fail to perform the whole he was ordered to add to the number of lashes in proportion to the failure, and still to add the deficiency to the next day's labor ; and thus he was daily to increase both the labor and stripes in case of failure. The overseer, hard-hearted as he was, expostulated with him, and assured him that the labor was more than the girls were able to perform, but he swore with a tremendous oath that they should do it or die. The poor creatures commenced the dreadful task, but being unaccustomed to such labor, their hands were soon worn to the quick; this they endured with patience, and did all they could to perform what was assigned them, but they were totally unable to accomplish it; they failed on the first day and recived the cruel lashes. The next morning with sore backs and bleeding hands they attempted the enlarged task — their hoe-handles were soon made red with their innocent blood — they labored with great assiduity, but they could not perform the unreasonable task, and consequently received the enlarged number of lashes. On the third morning they commenced again, but the task was so much enlarged that all hope of performing it was entirely precluded, and the enormously increased number of lashes became certain — the unhappy creatures despaired of life, and concluded that they must inevitably die under the torturing lash, unless they could despatch themselves in some other method. This appeared to be the only means of escaping the most terrible cruelty. Hence they formed and executed the dreadful design of hanging themselves. The horn blew for dinner, all started to their huts, but these unfortunate girls lingered behind, and unobserved by the rest of the company turned aside into a thicket, and there all six hanged themselves! They were soon missed, and search was quickly made for them — they were immediately found, and the cruel master, enraged by the disappointment and loss, made every possible exertion to bring them back to life, that they might again fall under the weight of his vengeance! but all his attempts were in vain — their souls were gone into awful eternity, and had their eternal destiny unalterably fixed! And being exceedingly exasperated on finding that they had escaped from his hand, he ordered a hole to be dug for them, and caused them to be tumbled into it like mere animal carcasses, while he vented the most awful imprecations upon them! And the overseer was ordered to exact from the rest of his slaves what labor he intended them to perform.

Thus we see that a single tyrant has driven six poor, helpless females out of life by exacting from them excessive labor. And who can estimate the sum of similar cruelties that are practiced upon the poor Africans, by the many thousand tyrants, who, from the slaveholding States, have literally received license for tyrannical exercise? To permit men to hold slaves is in reality the same thing as to give them license to commit cruelties, and those even of the most shocking kind. By such license the poor African girls we have just mentioned perished, and by it thousands are daily dropping into eternity from under the grievous burdens of excessive toil. That men will work their slaves to excess, must be expected when the inordinate love of gain is the predominating principle in the whole system of involuntary slavery. This principle induces many slaveholders to employ such overseers as are destitute of humane feeling, and naturally propense to cruelty, and thus well prepared to drive poor slaves to the highest degree of excessive labor. And in some instances they are given such an interest in the pending crops as stimulates them to the greatest severity in driving the miserable creatures whom they oversee. Thus the principles of avarice and cruelty in heaping most oppressive burdens of labor upon slaves, and that under such circumstances their situation is most deplorable, must be obvious to every one capable of reflection.

The same principle which induces some to place their slaves under the most merciless overseers, prompts others to take theirs to public places and let them for hire, to the highest bidders. In this way slaves often fall into the hands of the most cruel tyrants the world can produce, and consequently are most grievously oppressed by excessive labor — they must undergo whatever an insatiable avarice is pleased to lay upon them, and, like the ever yawning grave, it never says it is enough — it never compassionates the weary limbs of the poor enslaved Africans, nor proposes rest to those whom it chains down to servile life. It even drives them to the laborious task while they are sinking under the influence of mortal disease.

Those who are unacquainted with the depravity of the human heart, may be disposed to believe it impossible that any should be so cruel as to drive their slaves to work while they are laboring under mortal disease ; but it can be established by the best of testimony that slaves have been thus driven, and that almost to the moment of expiration !

A respectable gentleman, who is now a citizen of Flemingsburg, Fleming county, Kentucky, was, when in the State of South Carolina, invited by a slaveholder to walk with him and take a view of his farm. He complied with the invitation thus given, and in their walk they came to the place where the slaves were at work, and found the overseer whipping one of them very severely for not keeping pace with his fellows — in vain the poor fellow alledged that he was sick and could not work. The master seemed to think all was well enough, hence he and the gentleman passed on. In the space of an hour they returned by the same way, and found that the poor slave who had been whipped as they first passed by the field of labor, was actually dead ! This I have from unquestionable authority.

Thus we see that a merciless overseer will push his hapless slave for his labor, to the last moment, and follow him with the torturing lash into the very gates of eternity !

Similar cruelty has happened in Kentucky. In that State an unfeeling woman compelled a female slave to labor during the space of four days after she had received the mortal attack ! Thus are the poor creatures driven while their mortal frames are able to move. And the manner in which they are often treated after they are so reduced by disease as to be no longer able to move, is equally cruel.

A respectable physician of my acquaintance and now residing in the State of Alabama, did in that State attend upon twenty slaves, who were confined by severe fevers, and that in an open pen without roof, and thus were exposed to every shower of rain that fell during the time of their sickness.

This seems to be almost incredible ; but the source from which I have it is so unquestionable as to remove from my mind every doubt of its truth.

You may soon expect to hear from me again.

I AM YOURS, &c.

LETTER VIII.

DEAR BROTHER:

I design, in the present letter, to remark upon the extent of the slaveholder's power in relation to the infliction of corporeal punishments.

It is undeniable that the proprietors of slaves may punish them in any manner which a cruel spirit of revenge may dictate, provided they do not break limbs or take life. Hence they may torture them extremely during many years, and cause them to endure more than a thousand ordinary deaths, and yet neither take life nor even break a limb. Hence, I apprehend, there never has been among men a law productive of more misery than the one which permits men not merely to enslave, but even torture their fellow-creatures according to the dictates of every vengeful passion. I cannot express the indignation which I feel, when contemplating the injustice and cruelty of this detestable law. I abhor it more than I do the most loathsome carcass, and I detest all who, either in theory or practice, give it their sanction. But I am too passionate ; let me recall this harsh expression, which has been dictated by the tumultuous passions of my soul, aroused to the highest pitch of indignant feeling by the horrible scenes of cruelty that were presented to my mind! My flighty imagination added much to the tumult of passion by persuading me, for the moment, that I myself was a slave, and with my wife and children placed under the reign of terror. I began in reality to feel for myself, my wife, and my children — the thoughts of being whipped at the pleasure of a morose and capricious master, aroused the strongest feelings of resentment ; but when I fancied that the cruel lash was approaching my wife and children, and my imagination depicted in lively colors, their tears, their shrieks, and bloody stripes, every indignant principle of my nature was excited to the highest degree, and I could not well avoid execrating the law that permitted such injustice and cruelty, and my soul detested all who either in theory or practice gave it their sanction. But my mind has now returned from its reverie, and I find that these dreadful sufferings are not so near home as I had imagined — the enslaved Africans have to endure them, and not I and my family, and therefore my boisterous feelings are sinking into a calm, and I begin to lament my harshness — and you, my brother, will readily forgive it, if you will but bring the subject home to yourself by imagining that you are a slave, and, as such, subjected to the unrelenting lash of a cruel master, who delights to show his authority, and to treat you with the utmost indignity. And unless you will do this I am afraid you will be often offended with my warmth and severity. We are naturally too callous to the sufferings of others, and consequently prone to look upon them with cold indifference, until, in imagination we identify ourselves with the sufferers, and make their sufferings our own. And the moment we do this, our whole nature teems with sympathy, our feelings become impetuous, and the wings of passion bear us away to the abodes of suffering humanity, there to administer relief. When I look upon slavery as a distant thing, and inflicted upon an indifferent race of beings, it seems to wear a tolerable aspect; but when I bring it near, inspect it closely, and find that it is inflicted on men and women who possess the same nature and feelings with myself, my sensibility is immediately roused — but when I, who sustain the relations of husband and father, see a husband and father whipped severely in the presence of his wife and children, and that perhaps merely to gratify the caprice of an ill-natured master, my feelings become indignant; and when I see the mother most cruelly scourged in the presence of her husband and children, my feelings grow intolerable — my soul sickens at the sight, and my indignation almost prompts me to unlawful deeds of vengeance. But how can I quell my tumultuous passions, when, in addition to all this, I see the poor little children whipped in the presence of their parents, until their little backs are literally covered with blood? Had you, my brother, to endure all these cruelties, would you not abhor the law that permitted them to be inflicted upon you? And would you not detest all the people, who, either in theory or practice, gave it their sanction? Indeed, such a law must appear most detestable to every one that views it in its real nature and tendency — it sanctions the most tragical scenes of cruelty ever witnessed among men — it permits the slaveholder to bind his fellow-man, strip him naked, and whip him on the bare skin, with the keenest whips that art can invent, and that just so long as the most vengeful passion may dictate, provided the life is spared! Hence many poor slaves are stript naked, stretched and tied across barrels, or large logs, and tortured with the keenest lashes, during hours and even whole days, until their flesh is mangled to the very bones. Others are stript and hung up by the arms, their feet are tied together, and the end of a heavy piece of timber is put between their legs in order to stretch their bodies, and so prepare them for the torturing lash — and in this situation they are often whipt until their bodies are covered with blood and mangled flesh, and in order to add the greatest keenness to their sufferings, their wounds are washed with liquid salt! And some of the miserable creatures are permitted to hang in that position until they actually expire; some die under the lash, others linger about for some time, and at length die of their wounds, and many survive, and endure again similar torture. These bloody scenes are constantly exhibited in every slaveholding country — thousands of whips are every day stained in African blood! Even the poor females are not permitted to escape these shocking cruelties. Of this I will give you an instance.

A certain citizen of Kentucky purchased a piece of furniture, and after he brought it home, his wife unfortunately broke some small part of it, and that in the presence of a neighboring gentleman; she, nevertheless, charged it upon a black girl of about seventeen years of age. The girl honestly declared her innocence, but the mistress persisted in her charge against her. At length the brutish master seized the poor unfortunate girl, drew her clothes up over her head, hanged her by them to the limb of a tree, and in that shameful position whipt her several times very severely. By the extremity of torture she was sometimes forced to say that she did break the furniture, but in the moment of respite, she would honestly deny it again — and this subjected her to more torture. Fortunately for the poor girl the gentleman who was present when the woman broke the furniture, happened to be passing by; he paused in amazement at the shocking scene — he soon discovered the cause of the cruelty; indignation overcame him; he approached the brutish master, and told him that his own wife had broken the furniture in his presence, and declared that if he did not cease from torturing the poor girl he would give him as much as he had given her; with this the shameless monster thought it necessary to comply, and for that time the poor girl was released from his torturing hand. The gentleman who rescued the girl and stated this fact, is now a resident of the State of Ohio, and is known to be a man of truth.

It is painful to my feelings to record such a shameful outrage upon decency and humanity; but it is necessary to do it in order to show the horrible extent of the slaveholder's power over his slaves. Every slaveholder has power to strip his female slaves, and treat them in the same disgraceful manner, and thousands of them are base enough to put such power into exercise. It really grieves me to think that any government, and much more that our own, does sanction such an abomination.

Finally, our system of slavery puts it completely in the power of the slaveholders to dismember their slaves, or even murder them at pleasure! It is true that slaveholding States have enacted laws to prohibit the proprietors of slaves from breaking their limbs or taking their lives; but what avail such laws while slaves are made the property of their masters? May not men order their property to any place to which they may wish it to go? Hence, may not the vengeful master order his slave into his kitchen, or some other secret place, and there break all his limbs, tear out his eyes, and even murder him with the most savage cruelty? Or may he not do all this, even in the open field, in the presence of a thousand other slaves, and yet escape the sentence of the law? Not one of all this thousand could be a witness against him, and perhaps not one of them would even so much as dare to mention the crime. Hence, the poor slave has no security, either for his limbs or his life, further than what is in the will of his master. And, alas! there is often but little there. Could you secretly attend the fields, the kitchen, and the huts in which slaves labor and live, you would see limbs broken, skulls fractured, and even eyes torn out. And what is, if possible, still worse, you would see many most cruelly murdered.

A respectable young lady of my acquaintance, received a most painful shock by unexpectedly discovering one of the terrible things which are sometimes done in the kitchen. She visited the house of a certain Kentuckian, who was considered reputable. There she seemed at first to enjoy a pleasant hour in the social circle. In the parlor everything appeared comfortable and decent — every countenance was so cheerful that one might have imagined that good nature and happiness resided in the bosom of each member of the family. But, alas ! she unfortunately stepped into the kitchen. And, ah ! how changed was the scene. The most doleful aspect saluted her delicate eyes ; there sat a poor old black woman with one of her eyeballs hanging on her cheek ! it had been torn from the socket by the hand of her mistress ! how painful was the sight, and how doleful was the tale of wo ! and how little did the young visitant expect to witness such a scene ! She could not conceal her feelings — she wept, and she retired with emotions of horror ! This shocking cruelty was committed with impunity — no law could possibly reach the case. The tale of the poor sable sufferer would not be heard in court, and such crimes are seldom perpetrated in the presence of such as would be heard ; and when they are, but few if any are willing to be at the expense and trouble of commencing and supporting a prosecution on the behalf of slaves. The truth is, when once a man is made the property of another, and thus put completely under his control, it is impossible to enact laws that will protect either his life or his limbs. And every attempt to punish the master for abusing the slave will but instigate him to greater cruelty ! The love of gain affords all the protection the poor slaves can have, and it is well known that this has but little influence on the violent passions of men — to the vicious heart revenge is gain.

In spite of all law, slaveholders have the power of life and death over their slaves. And some of them do exercise such power with perfect impunity. It is undeniable that some drive their slaves nearly naked through frost and snow until they perish with cold ; some gradually starve them to death ; and some cause them to expire beneath the burden of excessive toil ; others whip them to death in a manner that more than equals the cruelty of the most barbarous savages ; and not a few murder them with clubs, axes and guns, or such like fatal weapons ! It is undeniable, that in these several ways many slaves are murdered with the utmost impunity ! It is seldom that even so much as a prosecution is incurred by murdering them ; and I do not recollect of ever hearing of a single individual being executed for taking the life of his slave. I am persuaded there is as much humane feeling in Fleming county, Kentucky, as can be found in any slaveholding section of country, of the same extent, and I think this will be readily admitted by all who are acquainted with the people of that county ; and yet there is a certain individual, in consequence of an unjust suspicion, fell upon his poor old slave, beat him in the face, and mashed it in such a manner as soon terminated his life; yet by it he incurred not even so much as a prosecution ! I mention this case, not because it is either singular or novel, but because it happened in one of the most humane sections of one of the mildest slaveholding countries, and therefore, is well calculated to show what is the real state of things, even where slavery wears its mildest aspect. It shows clearly that the system of slavery in its best form is fraught with the most horrid murders.

I will close this part of my subject by giving you an account of the most terrible display of slaveholding power, one that ought to make every slaveholding nation tremble, and one that must fill every humane bosom with horror! I will give it just as I received it from the pen of the Rev. William Dickey, who is well acquainted with the circumstances which he describes, and who is a man of undoubted veracity.

"In the county of Livingston, Ky., near the mouth of the Cumberland, lived Lilburn Lewis, a sister's son of the venerable Jefferson. He, who 'suckled at fair Freedom's breast,' was the wealthy owner of a considerable number of slaves, whom he drove constantly, fed sparingly, and lashed severely. The consequence was, they would run away. This must have given to a man of spirit and a man of business great anxieties until he found them, or until they had starved out and returned. Among the rest was an ill-grown boy about seventeen, who having just returned from a skulking spell, was sent to the spring for water, and in returning let fall an elegant pitcher. It was dashed to shivers upon the rocks. This was the occasion. It was night, and the slaves all at home. The master had them collected into the most roomy negro-house, and a rousing fire made. When the door was secured, that none might escape, either through fear of him or sympathy with George, he opened the design of the interview; namely, that they might be effectually taught to stay at home and obey his orders. All things being now in train, he called up George, who approached his master with the most unreserved submission. He bound him with cords, and by the assistance of his younger brother, laid him on the broad bench or meat-block. He now proposed to WHANG off George by the ancles!! It was with the broad axe! — In vain did the unhappy victim SCREAM AND ROAR; he was completely in his master's power. Not a hand amongst so many durst interfere. Casting the feet into the fire, he lectured them at some length. He WHACKED HIM OFF below the knees! George roaring out, and praying his master to BEGIN AT THE OTHER END! He admonished them again, throwing the legs into the fire! Then above the knees, tossing the joints into the fire! He again lectured them at leisure. The next stroke severed the thighs from the body. These were also committed to the flames. And so off the arms, head and trunk until all was in the fire! still protracting the intervals with lectures, and threatenings of like punishment in case of disobedience and running away, or disclosure of this tragedy. Nothing now remained but to consume the flesh and bones; and for this purpose the fire was briskly stirred until two hours after midnight, when, as though the earth would cover out of sight the nefarious scene, and as though the great Master in Heaven would put a mark of his displeasure upon such monstrous cruelty, a sudden and surprising shock of earthquake overturned the coarse and heavy back wall, composed of rock and clay, which completely covered the fire, and the remains of George. This put an end to the amusement of the evening. The negroes were permitted to disperse, with charges to keep this matter among themselves, and never to whisper it in the neighborhood under the penalty of a like punishment. When he retired, the lady exclaimed, 'Oh, Mr. Lewis, where have you been, and what have you done!' She had heard a strange pounding, and dreadful screams, and had smelt something like fresh meat burning! He said that he had never enjoyed himself at a ball so well as he had enjoyed himself that evening. Next morning he ordered the negroes to rebuild the back wall, and he himself superintended the work, throwing the pieces of flesh that still remained with the bones behind it as it went up, thus hoping to conceal the matter. But it could not be hid; much as the negroes seemed to hazard, they whispered the horrid deed to the neighbors, who came and before his eyes tore down the wall, and finding the remains of the boy they testified against him. But before the court sat, to which he was bound over, he was, by an act of suicide, with George in the eternal world.

Sure there are bolts red with no common wrath to blast the man. WILLIAM DICKEY.

Bloomingsburg, Oct. 8, 1824.

N. B. This happened in 1811, if I be correct, the 16th of December. It was the Sabbath!"

This awful scene of cruelty exhibits what tremendous things the slaveholder may do! And though the dreadful wretch was taken up on suspicion, and bound over to court, yet I apprehend there was little probability of his actually falling under the sentence of the law.* He might have eventually so managed the matter as to make the sentence fall upon the heads of his slaves. But be that as it might, it is certain that the State, by making men his property, gave him the opportunity of perpetrating the horrid deed, and therefore it stands first in the list of crimes!

FROM YOUR AFFECTIONATE BROTHER.

* This apprehension is rendered very probable by the fact that the populace actually let him out of prison in order to screen him from justice.

LETTER IX.

KIND BROTHER:

In the preceding letters I believe it is clearly shown, that involuntary slavery is opposed to the strongest principles and feelings of human nature, and if so, it forms a relation for which the God of nature, in the organization of the human system, has made no provision; and it appears to me self-evident that a relation so unnatural must be a constant source of misery to the several parties it unites. I invited your attention to its dreadful effects upon the party enslaved, while I was pointing out the extent of the slaveholder's power; and I shall now proceed to notice its tendency in respect to the enslaving party.

I. It is opposed to domestic peace. Slaves, as we have before shown, are generally raised without moral instruction, and consequently possess a low degree of moral feeling, and therefore they are not very conscientious in regard to the preservation of domestic peace. And a variety of families and individuals of different habits and feelings are crowded together in such a manner as is calculated to produce fierce contention. This disturbs the peace of the master's own family, and so becomes a source of perpetual vexation.

Again, slaves generally consider that they are laboring for others and not for themselves, and therefore they will avoid performing the labor assigned them as much as they can with safety to their backs, and even what they do is seldom done in a suitable manner. These things are a constant source of provocation to masters and overseers, and often instigate them to the greatest outrage and cruelty.

And we may further remark that slaves are generally but little influenced by the principles either of honor or piety, and consequently they often give themselves up to the practice of intemperance, falsehood, treachery, dishonesty and lewdness; and all these vices are frequently made to bear upon the master's family in such a manner as entirely banishes domestic peace. Thus a variety of circumstances conspire to deprive slaveholding families of that peace which is most essential to happiness, and the more they enslave and oppress their fellow-creatures, the more they increase their own disquietude and misery.

II. Idleness is generally one result of slavery. Necessity is the parent of industry — few are willing to labor when necessity does not impel them; and slaveholding families seldom feel the influence of this impelling principle. Consequently, where slaveholding parents feel disposed to raise their children to habits of industry, they generally find it exceedingly difficult, and in many instances totally impracticable. Children, in slaveholding countries, early imbibe the sentiment that work is the business of slaves, and that for free people to labor is of course disgraceful. This pernicious sentiment soon finds its way through the whole slaveholding community. Hence parents cannot brook the idea of shoving their children down to the rank of slaves, by making them labor. And the consequence of this is soon strongly manifested by the conduct of the rising family. The young masters cannot deign to pollute their hands with domestic concerns — and when they wish to ride abroad, their horses must be equipped and brought to the door, and the stirrups held by the humble slave while the young gallants mount. And should the delicate young misses sweep the house, or carry a bucket of water, they would scarcely be able to survive the disgrace!

These gentry despise and treat with contempt the laboring class of the community. They consider them to be no better than slaves, and therefore will not admit them to the privileges of equals; and in consequence of this many become ashamed to labor. Hence some who are scarcely able to procure bread, hire slaves to do the very labor which they might, and ought, but are ashamed to do themselves. I know by actual observation that this is true. And I presume that none who are acquainted with the slaveholding States will deny that slavery tends to idleness.

III. Slavery promotes vice among the free inhabitants of slaveholding States. By producing idleness it affords the opportunity of practicing immorality. Those who are closely engaged in useful occupations have little time for the practice of vice, but those who are idle have ample time for obeying the calls of every vicious appetite and passion, and consequently soon become a prey to their corrupt inclinations. Hence we may always expect to find the most confirmed habits of vice where idleness prevails.

Again, slaves, in consequence of the manner in which they are raised, are generally prone to vicious indulgence, and many of them are exceedingly profligate; their master's children often mingle with them, and not only witness their vicious practices, but also listen to lascivious conversation, and thus from infancy they become familiar with almost everything wicked and obscene. And this in connection with easy access, becomes a strong temptation to lewdness. Hence it often happens that the master's children practice the same vices which prevail among his slaves! and even the master himself is liable to be overwhelmed by the floods of temptation. And in some instances the father and his sons are involved in one common ruin; nor do the daughters always escape this impetuous fountain of pollution. Were it necessary I could refer you to several instances of slaves actually seducing the daughters of their masters! Such seductions sometimes happen even in the most respectable slaveholding families.

Further, slaves that are closely driven can earn much more than the coarse food and raiment which they eat and wear; and therefore, by becoming a source of gain, they afford the means of vicious indulgence. Hence gaming and intemperance are often the products of slavery. It is well known that a vast number derive such profit from the labor of their slaves, as enables them to devote their time to gaming, lewdness and intemperance. This class often give their whole attention to the practice and propagation of vice, and thus spread their baneful influence over the whole face of society. Hence it appears to me that if a State were to design the propagation of immorality, it could scarcely devise a better plan for the accomplishment of such design than is that of our present system of slavery. It implants the principles of vice in children as soon as their minds are capable of rational exercise; it cultivates them in the season of youth, and affords them the means of luxuriant growth in mature age.

IV. Slavery debilitates the constitution of slaveholding people. Man was formed for action, and therefore exercise is as necessary to his health as food is to his life; when he becomes inactive the powers of his nature languish, and debility pervades his whole constitution. Hence, in order to call man forth to action the beneficent Creator formed the earth for culture, and beneath its surface deeply buried the richest treasures. But slavery violates the plan of infinite wisdom by dooming some to excessive toil, while it releases others from the healthful field of exercise, and thus gives them over to debility, sickness and death. And in connection with this, we may further observe, that so far as slavery promotes lewdness, luxury and intemperance, it must have a most debilitating effect upon the constitution. And under the operation of such effects every slaveholding people must ultimately become sickly and short-lived.

V. Slavery must eventually tend to poverty. Slaveholders will engross large quantities of land, and this, in a great measure, will prevent the poorer class of people from acquiring real estates, or even a comfortable subsistence. Hence, extreme poverty in many instances must be inevitable. And even the richest slaveholders are not beyond the danger of poverty. Although great profit is often derived from the labor of slaves, yet that very profit frequently becomes the means of confirming such habits of gaming, intemperance and extravagance as eventually reduce the most wealthy to the most extreme indigence. To this we may add, that the children of the most wealthy slaveholders are generally raised to such idleness and extravagance as completely prepare them for squandering the estates left them by their parents; and consequently it often happens, that in a short time after they become masters of great estates, they are involved in the deepest poverty ; and finally become the most worthless vagabonds the world can produce.

We may further observe that in proportion as slaves increase, slaveholders will engross larger bodies of land, and of course there will be less room for free inhabitants ; therefore a diminution of the free population must be the certain result of the increase of slaves. And persons who are enslaved have not the same motives to industry which influence those who are free when they labor for themselves, and consequently they are not equal, in the performance of labor, to an equal number of free men. Hence, not only the poverty of individuals, but also that of the state must be the certain result of slavery. And when slaves become so numerous that there is not land enough for them to cultivate, extreme indigence must soon be the consequence, both to the State and individuals.

VI. Ignorance is another result of slavery. It is seldom that persons who are brought up in idleness and ease, will endure the labor necessary to a liberal education. They often drone out many long years at college, and return home mere quacks in learning. They cannot be induced to make that application which is necessary in the pursuit of science. They have generally a much stronger propensity for pleasure and amusement, than for the acquirement of useful knowledge. And in addition to this, they have too high an opinion of their own dignity to submit to the government of well-regulated seminaries. They often take offence at the very best regulations, and consequently desert the means of a good education. And in some cases it is necessary to expel them from institutions of learning, in consequence of their vicious habits and ungovernable tempers. Thus a propensity for idleness, the love of pleasure, vicious habits and untractable dispositions all conspire to prevent the slaveholding community from making progress in the paths of science. And though some noble minds may occasionally stem these difficulties, and climb to the highest eminence in learning, yet the great mass of the people will be more liable to retrograde than to advance in literature.

VII. Slavery weakens every State in which it exists. Slaveholders, as we before stated, will engross large bodies of land, and this of course leaves less room for free citizens, who, having to labor for the sustenance of themselves and their families, are despised and shoved down to a rank little above that of slaves ; this becomes to them a strong inducement to move into free States, where they can be admitted to an equal rank with their fellow-citizens. We may further add, that many of the very best citizens of the slaveholding States are conscientiously opposed to slavery, and fully apprized of its pernicious tendency upon society in general and particularly upon the rising generation ; and therefore, in order to save their offspring from temptation and impending ruin, they move into the free States where they may more easily train up their children to industry and morality. And besides all this, slavery is the means of promoting lewdness, intemperance and luxury, by which thousands of the free inhabitants perish. Under the operation of these several causes every slaveholding State must grow weaker in proportion as the slave population increases. Slaves know they ought to be free, and therefore may be expected to embrace the first opportunity of breaking the yoke of bondage. This is fully established by the many insurrections that take place in various slaveholding countries ; hence almost every slave is to be considered an internal enemy. And in some States the slave population is already more extensive than the free, and is still rapidly increasing ; and must therefore soon become able, without foreign assistance, to overpower their oppressors. And it is obvious that persons raised in idleness, luxury and ease, are but little calculated for making powerful resistance, and therefore must become an easy prey to their enemies. From all these circumstances we may safely conclude that all the slaveholding States will eventually become dependent on the free States for protection, both from their slaves and foreign invasion. Slaveholding States never can be powerful in war. Those who are unaccustomed to labor cannot endure the fatigue of a campaign, and being habituated to commanding they are seldom willing to be commanded, and therefore are likely to become a prey to their own rashness. This doubtless occasioned some of the misfortunes of the Kentuckians during the last war. They were brave, but ungovernable; hence they fell into the hand of the enemy.

VIII. Slavery cultivates a spirit of cruelty. Slaves consider themselves unjustly enslaved, and consequently they often neglect and slight the service assigned them ; this instigates the master to cruelty. And indeed many of the poor creatures, in consequence of the want of moral instruction, are so vicious as to elicit cruel treatment even from the most humane. Thus the children of slaveholders from infancy have the opportunity of becoming familiar with scenes of cruelty. This has a tendency to blunt the tender sensibilities of their nature, to make them think lightly of human misery, and fully prepare them for cruel indulgence when they arrive at mature age. Therefore it is obvious that a disposition to cruelty must in some measure pervade every slaveholding community.

IX. Slavery tends to tyranny.* It is directly opposed to those fundamental principles of republi-

* The children of slaveholders are, in many instances, habituated to tyrannizing over slaves. This cultivates in them the spirit of tyranny. In this respect slavery has a most direct tendency to make tyrants.

canism maintained in that part of the Declaration of Independence, which declares, 'That all men are created equal; that they are endowed by their Creator with certain inalienable rights; that among these are life, liberty and the pursuit of happiness,' These principles are absolutely denied by the slaveholding States. They practically declare that all men are not created equal, that liberty is not an inalienable right, and that a certain class of people have not a right to pursue their own happiness. They do in their constitutions create distinctions among men; some they forever consign to the service of others. They tell us 'That no freeman ought to be taken or imprisoned, or deprived of his freehold, liberties, or privileges, or outlawed, or exiled, or in any manner destroyed, or deprived of his life, liberty, or property, but by the judgment of his peers, or by the law of the land.' [See the constitutions of Maryland, N. and S. Carolina, and Tennessee.] This plainly implies that the slave ought to be taken, imprisoned and destroyed without either judgment or law. The constitution of Kentucky tells us, 'That all freemen when they form a social compact are equal.' [See the constitution of Kentucky, Art. X. Sec. I.] Kentucky cannot admit 'That all are created equal,' nor that even freemen are equal until they become so by social compact. Thus she plainly denies a fundamental principle of the Declaration of Independence. And how widely does she differ from the free States, which declare in their constitutions 'That all men are born equally free and independent.' There is no State in the Union that makes stronger pretensions to republicanism than does Kentucky, and yet she both theoretically and practically denies the fundamental principle upon which the whole republican system rests. The truth is, all the slaveholding States do practically maintain the fundamental principles of absolute monarchy—which are, that all men are not equal, and that all men are not born equally free and independent. Every slaveholder is an absolute monarch to his slaves, and they are bound to approach him with all the sensibilities of inferiority which absolute monarchy can require. And many slaveholders do manifest by their conduct that they feel the same superiority over their poor slaves that absolute monarchs do over their miserable and abject subjects.

It is well known that the slaveholding States have, ever since the Declaration of Independence, manifested a propensity for the unjust acquisition of power. They have ever had an unequitable representation in Congress. They consider slaves to be mere property, and yet for every seventy thousand of them they claim the right of sending one representative to Congress. This is decidedly a representation of property. The slave representation is as unjust and unreasonable as a cattle representation would be. Did they permit the poor slaves to choose for themselves a representation which might contend for their rights in the national legislature, none would have reason to reproach them for injustice with respect to such representation. But, alas! the slave representation is for a far different purpose. It is to strengthen the yoke and tighten the chains of cruel oppression. But the slave representation appears to me still more unjust, when I consider that the States which hold the greatest number of slaves, and of course have the greatest slave representation, must be of the least service for the defence of the nation in time of war. They have many voices, and of course are immensely powerful in the national legislature, but are perfect weakness in the field of battle—perhaps it requires all their strength to keep their slaves in subjection.

The tenacity with which the slaveholding States retain this unjust principle manifests a strong propensity for the usurpation of power. And this circumstance shows that they have in them the spirit of tyranny.

Now brother, I think it must be evident to you that slavery, in the several particulars to which I have invited your attention, has a pernicious tendency upon the free inhabitants of the slaveholding States; and hence you have another conclusive proof that slavery is opposed to the natural principles and feelings of our nature, and that of course, as we said before, it forms a relation for which the Creator, in the organization of the human system, has made no provision. From the plain principles of nature as well as from its dreadful tendency, it evidently appears that involuntary slavery is both unnatural and unjust.

In my next, I intend to investigate the title by which slaves are held in servitude. ADIEU.

LETTER X.

AFFECTIONATE BROTHER:

According to promise, I am now to enter upon the investigation of the title by which slaves are held in servitude.

It must be admitted that the Africans and the rest of mankind have all sprung from one common father; and consequently all originally were alike free. It will also be admitted that the Africans were not enslaved for crime; hence we conclude with the utmost certainty that they were unjustly enslaved. They must have been taken either by theft or open violence, and sold into slavery; therefore it inevitably follows that the title to them was originally derived from those who either stole them or took them by unjust violence, and sold them into bondage; consequently it must be most unjust; nor neither time, nor custom, nor government can change its nature — it stands in eternal opposition to right. Property that is stolen or taken by unjust violence, though it pass through a thousand hands by honest purchase, still belongs to the original owner; and to him, according to the plainest principles of justice, it must revert. The right to freedom belongs to the Africans, and therefore it is as unjust to hold it from them as it is to hold stolen property from its right owner. Suppose that your little daughter were to be stolen in her infantile state and sold for a slave, would she not, according to the plainest principles of justice, be as much entitled to freedom as she now is? Again, suppose that an unjust and arbitrary power should detain her posterity in slavery to a thousand generations, would not the last generation be as much entitled to freedom as the mother originally was? Do you believe that any one would be just in depriving them of their right to freedom, merely because he had purchased them from those who had no right to sell them? No; you certainly believe that it would be most unjust. Now this is precisely the situation of the Africans you hold in servitude. Their ancestors were originally free; but were unjustly taken and sold into bondage, and by an unjust and arbitrary power their offspring are still enslaved. You suppose that you have a right to them by honest purchase, but they are the same as stolen property. The title to them was originally derived from the hand of the thief. Hence the man from whom you purchased them had no just title to them, of course had no right to sell them ; you had no right to buy them ; and consequently can have no right to detain them in servitude. The right to freedom is original in all the human race. 'That all men are created equal' is a truth that no true-hearted republican will deny. Hence, while you hold slaves, you hold the right of freedom from its real owners. And is not freedom more precious than property? And therefore is it not more criminal to hold it from your fellow-creatures than it is to deprive them of their property ? How then can you persist in holding them as slaves, merely because you purchased them from such as had no right to sell them ? Should you purchase a stolen horse, would you pretend to keep him from his real owner, merely because you had purchased him from the thief who had stolen him ? No, you would certainly give him up to the real proprietor as soon as he should exhibit sufficient evidence of the justness of his claim. Then why not deliver up to your slaves their liberty, seeing they are undoubtedly entitled to freedom ? We, as a nation, in our Declaration of Independence, have declared that the right to liberty is unalienable. I know the laws of your State permit you to enslave a certain class of your fellow-creatures ; but the permission of a State cannot change moral principle. Should this State permit you to enslave my children, would it be honest in you to take advantage by such permission to make them slaves ? Certainly you must admit, that to take such advantage would be both unjust and cruel. And is it not equally unjust and cruel to enslave the poor Africans, merely because the State gives permission for such oppression? The man who will be just no farther than the State compels him, is a rogue in heart. And the man who will take away the liberty of another whenever the State permits him, would also take the property of another if similar permission was granted him. I do not say that all slaveholders are rogues in heart. I hope many of them have acted more from mistake than from real dishonesty. But I do not hesitate in saying that they all unjustly take away the liberty of their fellow creatures, who, according to the principles admitted by our nation, 'were born equally free and independent.'

I shall next attempt, by the scriptures, to prove the injustice of involuntary slavery.

FAREWELL.

LETTER XI.

LOVING BROTHER:

According to an intimation given in my last, I am to show that the modern system of slavery is prohibited by the book of inspiration. And as many of the abettors of this system pretend to support it by the sacred Scriptures, I deem it necessary to examine the principal arguments which they have drawn from this source.

I. I shall first consider the one which is founded upon Noah's curse. It is argued that this curse consigns all the posterity of Ham to perpetual slavery; that the Africans descended from him; and therefore it is right to enslave them.

I consider that this argument is, in several respects, ill founded.

First, it is not true that the curse consigns all the posterity of Ham to perpetual servitude. Let us hear what it says. (Gen. ix. 25.) 'Cursed be Canaan; a servant of servants shall he be unto his brethren.' Thus we see that but one of Ham's sons was included in the curse. Canaan, doubtless was deeply concerned with his father in the guilt which gave rise to this denunciation against him, else why was he so signally marked as the subject of the curse? The rest of Ham's sons it seems were innocent, and consequently were not included in it. The history of the world shows that many of the nations which descended from them have been respectable, and subjected to no calamities but such as are common to the rest of mankind. Hence it is as plain as stubborn fact can make it, that the curse did not include all of Ham's posterity. It was denounced against Canaan, and history shows that it fell upon his posterity. Our Africans did not descend from him, and therefore were not with him consigned to servitude.

2d. The doom was not perpetual. Sacred history shows that the descendants of Canaan became powerful and wealthy nations before the curse was inflicted upon them. It was first inflicted by the Israelites, who descended from Shem, and who had been servants to some of Ham's posterity in Egypt. They destroyed vast numbers of the Canaanites, and eventually reduced the rest of them to very abject circumstances, and made them tributary. And thus they became the tributary servants of those who had been servants. Hence the following predictions of Noah were literally fulfilled. 'Cursed be Canaan; a servant of servants shall he be unto his brethren.'

'Blessed be the Lord God of Shem; and Canaan shall be his servant.'

Again, it is said Japhet 'shall dwell in the tents of Shem; and Canaan shall be his servant.' This was doubtless accomplished when the Greeks and Romans, who were descendants of Japhet, by conquest took possession of the tents of Shem. At this period the remnant of the Canaanites became tributary to the offspring of Japhet, and thus Canaan became the servant of Japhet. Hence the prediction, so far as it related to servitude, has long since had its accomplishment. The Canaanites have mingled with other nations, and so do not now exist as a distinct people, and consequently the term of their servitude must be terminated. And when we consider the manner in which these ancient predictions were fulfilled, we believe that they related not so much to the slavery of individuals as to national subjugation. There were so few of Canaan's posterity reduced to individual slavery, that we cannot reasonably conclude that to be the kind of servitude predicted. It appears from sacred history that fewer of the descendants of Canaan than those of Shem were reduced to individual slavery. People who are subjugated and made tributary, must labor in order to pay their tribute, and therefore are the servants of their conquerors. This kind of servitude the Canaanites endured to great extremes. The Israelites conquered them, and took possession of their cities, their houses, and their lands, and thus enjoyed the fruits of their labor; and those of them that escaped the sword were eventually made tributary. This evidently appears to be the kind of servitude predicted in Noah's curse, and if so, our kind of slavery is not even so much as found in this ancient prediction. The Israelites were not commanded to enslave, but to exterminate the nations of Canaan.

Finally, if the prediction had included all Ham's posterity, and had consigned them to perpetual servitude, still it could not justify our system of slavery. Predictions are not given in Scripture as rules of moral action. It was predicted, and even decreed, that Jesus Christ should be crucified, and yet his crucifiers were full as guilty as they would have been if no such prediction and decree had ever existed. The Israelites did not proceed against the Canaanites on the ground of prediction, but on that of divine command, and that command was not founded upon prediction, but upon the full cup of their iniquities. The Lord gave the Canaanites a dispensation of grace under the ministrations of Melchisedec, and suspended the infliction of the curse until they had long abused his mercy and filled full the cup of their iniquities. Hence, their enormous wickedness was the real cause of their calamities, and the means of bringing the curse upon them. But even on the supposition that this prediction were a rule of moral action, still it could not justify our system of slavery, because we have not sufficient proof that our Africans descended from Ham. We suppose they are of his posterity, but this supposition cannot be supported by satisfactory evidence. The revolutions of nations and time have put the matter beyond the possibility of certain proof. Therefore the whole argument for slavery drawn from Noah's curse, is without foundation. It rests wholly upon bold assertion and mere conjecture, and it certainly must be the product of avaricious derangement.

II. I shall consider the argument which the friends of involuntary slavery have adduced from the example of Abraham. It is alledged that Abraham, the father of the faithful, held slaves, and therefore involuntary slavery must be right.

This argument, like the one before considered, appears to me to be inconclusive in several respects.

First: It is not evident that Abraham's servants were held to involuntary servitude. It is true that he had servants born in his house, and servants bought with his money; but these circumstances do not absolutely prove that their servitude was involuntary. Abraham was a prince; the children of Heth addressed him as such; (Gen. xxiii. 6.) 'Thou art a mighty prince among us.' On one occasion he armed three hundred and eighteen trained servants that were born in his house, and with them gained a signal victory over several of the most powerful kings of the age. (Gen. xiv. 1—16.) Hence it appears that the servants born in his house were merely his subjects. Abraham had no fixed residence, and therefore he and his subjects dwelt in tents. 'By faith he sojourned in the land of promise, as in a strange country, dwelling in tabernacles with Isaac and Jacob.' (Heb. xi. 9.) Thus we see that Abraham's house was but a tabernacle or tent; and it was made large enough to shelter him and all his subjects; and this shows how it happened that the three hundred and eighteen before-mentioned servants were born in his house. These were all fit to bear arms; and therefore, according to the nature of human increase, we must conclude that Abraham had many others likewise born in his house, who were too young for military service, and there must have been nearly an equal number of females—and to all these we may add all those bought with his money. From these circumstances it is reasonable to conclude that Abraham's servants, at least, amounted to more than one thousand. Hence it is most absurd to suppose that a single individual while passing from place to place in a strange country, could compel so large a number of persons to involuntary servitude. And would any man in his senses, under such circumstances, arm three hundred and eighteen involuntary slaves, and march them out against his enemies? Would such a number of armed slaves submit to a single man, cheerfully fight his battles, and thus risk their lives in his defence? Abraham was a wandering stranger, unprotected by civil government, and therefore his servants were not restrained by fear of punishment in case of rebellion; consequently we may safely conclude that the service which they rendered him was of the voluntary kind. But the question still recurs, were not those whom he bought with his money slaves? To this I answer that 'Abraham was very rich in cattle, in silver, and in gold;' and was as benevolent as he was rich; of course he would have many strong inducements to redeem miserable captives taken in war; and these, from a sense of gratitude as well as for the sake of protection, would become his subjects; and such being redeemed by their own consent would be under the most solemn obligations to render him faithful service. Perhaps Hagar the Egyptian was bound to his service from some such consideration, and therefore was called a bond-woman. Indeed Abraham manifested so much benevolence in several instances, as might lead us to the conclusion that he was wholly indisposed to the practice of involuntary slavery. And his whole conduct towards his servants shows that he considered them to be merely subjects, and not slaves. Hence we find him bringing his eldest servant under solemn oath not to take a wife to Isaac of the daughters of the Canaanites. Gen. xxiv. 2, 3. This we might expect a prince to require of a subject, but not a master to require of a slave. This same servant had all his master's property in his hand ; and even had authority over Isaac. Does this look like modern slavery ? Thus a variety of circumstances make it evident to me that Abraham did not hold involuntary slaves. But again, if Abraham did practice involuntary slavery, still the argument adduced from his example must be inconclusive. He was an imperfect man, and therefore his example cannot be a standard of moral rectitude. He had two wives at one time ; but who will argue from his example that polygamy is right. And it must be equally absurd to argue from his example that slavery is right. Such an argument evidences a bad cause.

III. I shall examine the argument which the defenders of our slaveholding system have adduced from the Mosaic institutions.

This argument they consider as fully supported by Lev. xxv. 44, 45, 46. 'Both thy bond-men, and thy bond-maids, which thou shalt have, shall be of the heathen that are round about you ; of them shall ye buy bond-men and bond-maids. Moreover of the children of strangers that do sojourn among you, of them shall ye buy, and of their families that are with you, which they begat in your land : and they shall be your possession : and ye shall take them as an inheritance — for your children after you to inherit them for a possession ; and they shall be your bond-men forever ;* but over your brethren the children of Israel, ye shall not rule one over another with rigor.'

As this sacred passage is considered to be one of the strongest pillars upon which the modern

* This may mean that the Hebrews might keep up a succession of servants by successive purchase, and not that any individuals would be held in servitude forever.

system of slavery rests, it will be necessary to give it a careful and candid examination. Hence we remark,

First; That it gives to the children of Israel, by special grant, some of the heathen for slaves. This, it is thought, fully justifies our system of slavery; but I apprehend that the opposite is true. This special grant implies that the children of Israel without it had no right to enslave even the heathen. These were the property of the Creator; therefore none could have a right to possess them but by the special grant from him. The Israelites held slaves by special license from their Creator and real proprietor, and such special license amounts to a real prohibition of similar privilege to all to whom it is not given. When I, for instance, make grant of a certain piece of property, my conduct in that case plainly declares that I consider myself the real proprietor of that property, and that none have a right to it but by special title from me. And thus the special grant which God made of the heathen to the Israelites, shows plainly that he considered himself the real proprietor, and that none had a right to hold them as a possession but by special grant from him. No such grant has ever been made to any people, and therefore, the very text on which slaveholders rely for support, amounts to a real prohibition of slavery in all cases except the one which it specifies. Hence, do not modern slaveholders rob the Almighty while they hold his property for a possession? And 'Shall a man rob God and prosper?'

2d. The text specifies the character sustained by the persons consigned to servitude. They must not be servants of the true God, for of these the Lord says, 'They are my servants.—They shall not be sold as bond-men;' but they must be heathen ; that is, they must be idolators. Hence it is evident that they were enslaved for the crime of idolatry. And when they ceased to be heathen, embraced the true religion, and thus become the servants of Jehovah, they were entitled to the benefits of jubilee. The covenant made with Abraham required them to be circumcised, and of course to be taught the principles of true religion. (Gen. xvii. 18.) 'He that is born in thy house, and he that is bought with thy money must needs be circumcised.' The same is required in Exodus, xii. 44, 45. 'But every man's servant that is bought for money, when thou hast circumcised him, then shall he eat thereof. A foreigner and an hired servant shall not eat thereof.' And when servants, after being circumcised as members of a believer's household, made a full profession of their faith by eating the passover, they were to be considered the servants of God, and therefore were entitled to the privileges of Israelites, who, according to law, could not be enslaved ; 'But over your brethren, the children of Israel, ye shall not rule one over another with rigor.' And why ? Because 'they are my servants ;' and this reason was equally applicable to all professors of true religion. 'One law shall be to him that is home-born, and unto the stranger that sojourneth among you.' — 'And he shall be as one born in the land.' But to this it may be you will reply that the law expressly says, 'They shall be your bondmen forever,' and therefore their servitude was perpetual.

I readily admit that the words 'for ever' do, according to their primary signification, express endless duration, and that they are always to be thus understood when used in relation to eternal things ; but when used in relation to temporal things they are limited by the nature and circumstances of the subjects to which they relate. It is said in Exodus, xxi. 6, that a Hebrew servant, under the circumstances there mentioned, should serve his master 'for ever,' but according to another law he could not be made to serve longer than to the year of jubilee. And hence it is evident that the words are used in a figurative sense, and not in their original sense, and merely intended to express the duration of forty-nine years, the time between the years of jubilee; so I apprehend they are limited in respect to other servants, by the same law. 'And ye shall hallow the fiftieth year, and proclaim liberty throughout all the land, unto all the inhabitants thereof.' (Lev. xxv. 10.) According to this law, none could be enslaved longer than from the time they were purchased to the year of jubilee. Then liberty must be proclaimed to the captives. (Isa. lxi. 1.) Hence the slavery permitted by the Mosaic institutions was not similar to that which exists among us. It was for the punishment of idolatry; it was by divine permission, and it was not perpetual. The poor slave expected a year of universal liberation, a glorious emblem of the gospel-day. But the slavery among us is not for crime, is not by divine permission, and is perpetual. No joyful year of jubilee is now expected by the miserable slave! And even many of the servants of Jehovah are enslaved. Consequently the attempt to support our system of slavery by the Mosaic institutions is most absurd.

ADIEU.

LETTER XII.

DEAR BROTHER:

I shall in the present letter give you a few remarks upon the arguments which the Rev. Archibald Cameron, of Kentucky, has presented to the public in the first number of the Monitor, printed at Lexington, A. D. 1806. The reverend gentleman possesses both the talents and literature necessary to making the best of the cause he attempts to defend. And could we suppose him actuated by the unhallowed motives of self-interest, we would say he had from that source sufficient inducement to the greatest industry in the management of his subject ; for, as we understand, he had, and perhaps still has, considerable property in human flesh, and blood, and souls ! ! And it became him, as a public teacher to show, if possible that his practice was in accordance with the gospel. In short, we believe that if Mr. Cameron had been unsuccessful in adducing arguments to justify the practice of slavery, it was entirely owing to a bad cause, and not to the want of talents, literature, or industry.

His arguments are principally drawn from several passages in the New Testament in which servants are mentioned. He lays his strong foundation in the signification of the word DOULOS, which is translated into the word servant. He says, 'It is well known to those who are in the habit of reading the writings of the ancients, that DOULOS in Greek, the word used above, and *servus* in Latin, are used to signify that kind of servitude which is perpetual or for life, which we call slavery. ELUTHEROS, the Greek word for free, it set in opposition to DOULOS, servant, which shows that the Apostle meant a bondman, or a slave, when he used the term.'

This argument is plausible, but not solid. Paul says, 'Though I be (Elretheros) free from all men, yet (edoulosa) I have made myself servant unto all.' (1 Cor. ix. 19.) And he commands the Galatians (douleuete) to serve one another by love. (Gal. v. 13.) EDOULOSA signifies I have made myself (doulos) a servant ; and 'is set in opposition to ' (Elutheros) free ; but who would argue from this that Paul was an involuntary slave for life ? Yet such an argument would be just as conclusive as the one which Mr. Cameron has advanced in the passage we have quoted from the Monitor. I readily admit that the apostle had reference to some kind of servitude when he said, 'Art thou called, being (doulos) a servant, care not for it ; but if thou mayest be made (Elutheros) free, use it rather.' (1 Cor. vii. 21.) But there is no evidence from the language of the text what kind of servitude was meant. The Greek word DOULOS, like the English word servant, specifies no particular kind of servitude. Hence the translators have not, in a single instance, in all the New Testament, translated the word DOULOS into the word slave. The word slave is specific in its meaning, and always, except when used figuratively, denotes one bound to involuntary and perpetual servitude ; and in all its more general applications, it still refers to one particular kind of bondage. Every slave is a servant, but every servant is not a slave. All apprentices are servants, and actually bondmen during their apprenticeship, and are, in many instances, subjected to stripes ; but they are not called slaves. Hirelings are servants, and in some parts of the world even these have endured stripes; yet no accurate writer would call them slaves. The translators thought it proper to use the word slave in but a single instance, in all the New Testament. (Rev. xviii. 13.) 'Slaves and souls of men' are mentioned as the unhallowed merchandise of spiritual Babylon. And here the Greek word is not DOULOS but SOMATON, the genitive plural of SOMA. The truth is, the word DOULOS has such an extensive and various application in the sacred scriptures, that it would be very injudicious to translate it into a word so limited and determinate in its signification as is the word slave, which properly denotes a person bound to involuntary and perpetual servitude. DOULOS has no such definitive meaning, but answers to the English word servant, which is as applicable to the subject of a prince, to the common hireling, or even to the apprentice, as it is to the slave. In many instances it would be most ridiculous to translate DOULOS into slave, as a single specification will show. 'Paul (doulos) a slave of Jesus Christ.' How ridiculous is such a translation! Christ is 'The Prince of the Kings of the earth.' Paul is his servant, but not his involuntary slave. DOULOS is used in relation to the subjects of kings or nobles. (Luke xix. 17.) 'Well, thou good (doule) servant—have thou authority over ten cities.' Certainly the subject of a prince, and not a slave, must have been intended by DOULE in this passage. Who would imagine that authority over ten cities would be given to a slave? DOULOS is likewise used in relation to hired servants. The penitent prodigal said, 'How many (misthioi) hirelings, or hired servants of my father's have bread enough.' And again, when expressing his willingness to accept of the lowest station in his father's house, he said, 'I am no more worthy to be called thy son: make me as one of thy hired servants.' But the father said to his (doulos) servants, bring forth the best robe and put it on him. (Luke, xv. 11—32.) The prodigal said that the hirelings were his father's, and had bread enough and to spare. This would be quite unnatural, if there were still a lower order of servants in his father's house, and indeed would imply that such servants had not bread enough. Again, he says, make me as one of thy hirelings. This, on the supposition that there were still a lower order than these in his father's family, was as good as saying, I am not yet unworthy enough to take the lowest place in thy family; and would destroy both the beauty and fitness of the parable, which was intended to illustrate the nature of true repentance, and the willingness of our heavenly Father to receive the humble penitent. The truly penitent sinner is willing to take the lowest station in his father's house. But Mr. Cameron, contrary to the nature of the parable, supposes that the father of the prodigal held slaves; but upon such supposition the prodigal was very unlike the penitent sinner whom he was intended to represent. Hence it is evident that the father's (douloi) servants were his hirelings.

Once more. Doulos is used in relation to such as dedicate themselves to the service of others. So Paul, as we have already shown, made himself (doulos) a servant unto all. And so those who have dedicated themselves to the service of God are called his servants. (Rev. xxii. 3.) 'And his (douloi) servants shall serve him.' The elder brother of the prodigal is represented as saying to his father, 'Lo, these many years (doulueo) do I serve thee!' And our Lord says, 'Whosoever commiteth sin, is the (doulos) servant of sin.' (John viii. 34.) Paul also says, 'To whom ye yield yourselves (douloi) servants to obey, his (douloi) servants ye are.' (Rom. vi. 16.)

Consequently, Mr. Cameron must be mistaken when he says, 'that DOULOS in Greek—(IS) used to signify that kind of servitude which is perpetual or for life, which we call slavery.' It has no such definite signification; no difference whether a man serves voluntarily or involuntarily, whether he serves an hour or during life, he is (doulos) a servant during the time he serves. It is a general term which is equally applicable to all kinds of servants, without regard either to the nature or duration of their servitude. Hence, it affords no proof either for or against our present system of slavery. Thus far we think Mr. Cameron has failed in his arguments.

Again, Mr. Cameron, on pages 9th and 10th quotes 1 Tim. vi. 1, 2. 'Let as many servants as are under the yoke, count their own masters worthy of all honor; that the name of God and his doctrine be not blasphemed. And they that have believing masters, let them not despise them because they are brethren; but rather do them service because they are faithful and beloved partakers of the benefit.' He appears to be confident 'that this has a reference to slavery, or perpetual servitude.' And in connection with it, he tells us of an ancient custom of making captives pass under the yoke as a token of their subjection to slavery, that such 'Were sold and bought like other property,' and that of this description of persons the Apostle Paul says, 'Let as many servants as are (upozugon) under the yoke, count their own masters worthy of all honor.' But I see not the least evidence that the apostle had any reference to such custom. The apostle does not say, let as many servants as *have passed under the yoke*; but he says, 'Let as many servants as *are under* the yoke, count their own masters worthy of all honor.' The yoke which he mentions is not one under which they had passed; but one that was still upon them. And according to Mr. Cameron's own description of the instrument under which captives were made to pass, it is evident that the apostle had no reference to it as an emblem of perpetual slavery. In a note on the word yoke he says, 'JUGUM, a yoke, a contrivance with forks and spears, like a gallows, under which enemies vanquished were forced to go. Hence it is used to signify bondage or slavery.' But ZUGON, the word which the apostle uses, signifies no such kind of yoke as Mr. Cameron here describes; it is derived from the Greek verb ZEUGNUO, (I join together,) and consequently signifies an instrument of conjugation, such as the yoke which unites or couples oxen together; and because it thus couples them, it is called ZUGON, (a yoke); therefore, it is not the kind of instrument under which Mr. Cameron says captives were made to pass as an emblem of their being subjected to slavery. In allusion to the yoke which binds the ox to his fellow, bondage of various kinds is in the scriptures termed a yoke. Subjects are bound to obey their prince, and thus are under the yoke. (1 Kings, xii. 4.) 'Thy father (king Solomon) made our yoke grievous.' Christ is a king, and they that will be his subjects must take his yoke upon them — 'Take my yoke upon you — For my yoke is easy.' (Matt. xi. 29, 30.

Again, the husband is bound to the wife, and the wife to the husband; and though they be thus bound by voluntary engagement, and though their union be a source of their greatest happiness, yet they are under the yoke. Hence, Paul says, (2 Cor. vi. 14.) 'Be ye not unequally yoked together.' (Phil. iv. 3) 'I entreat thee, also, true yoke fellow.' This was a certain person who had voluntarily associated himself with Paul in propagating the gospel among the heathen.

These instances are sufficient to show that the word yoke is figuratively used as a general term, which is equally applicable to every kind of bondage. Mr. Cameron himself, on page 27th, admits that every 'obligation to virtue' is a yoke. He there argues that 'If the phrase every yoke, be not qualified and restricted, it will be proper to break asunder the yoke of Christianity, the yoke of the civil law, the yoke of marriage, and every other obligation to virtue.' Thus while he pleads for a limitation of the phrase 'every yoke,' he admits the universal application of the term yoke in respect to every 'obligation to virtue.' It is strange that he makes such admission, after limiting the term to perpetual and involuntary slavery. But what is still more strange, he first argues that the term yoke is applicable to slavery alone, when used by the Apostle in relation to servants; but when he is commanded to 'break every yoke,' (Isa. 58) he argues that the phrase 'every yoke' must be so 'qualified and restricted' as not to include slavery; else, he says, 'It will be proper to break asunder the yoke of Christianity, the yoke of civil law, the yoke of marriage, and every other obligation to virtue.' If the phrase 'every yoke' does not include slavery, I do not see how the phrase 'under the yoke' can signify slavery. That the apostle had reference to some kind of bondage when he used the phrase 'under the yoke,' I readily admit; but I see no evidence that he had reference to involuntary and perpetual slavery. Hired servants were in that age very numerous. The father of the prodigal is represented as having many of them in his service. The prodigal says, 'How many hired servants of my father's have bread enough.' And the Apostle James in his epistle severely reproves the rich for defrauding the laborers that had reaped their fields. (James v. 4.) 'Behold, the hire of the laborers who have reaped down your fields, which is of you kept back by fraud, crieth, and the cries of them which have reaped are entered into the ears of the Lord of Sabaoth.' This shows that the fields of the rich were generally reaped by hired servants, and not by slaves. Now, had slaves been so exceedingly numerous as Mr. Cameron, on page 11th, attempts, by profane history, to prove them to have been, the rich would have no need to hire reapers. If slaves were held they were held by the rich; but James, in a general epistle intended for the use of all the churches, represents the rich as hiring their reapers. This does not evidence that slaves were numerous. But had the rich generally held slaves, and treated them with so shocking cruelty as Mr. Cameron says they did, can we suppose that the agonizing cries of the poor slaves would not have 'entered into the ears of the Lord of Sabaoth,' as well as the cries of defrauded hirelings? Has the Almighty no compassion for the hapless slave? Surely the Sovereign of the universe is no respecter of persons, his compassion descends to the meanest of his creatures; the angel and the worm are alike the subjects of his care. Hence it is most reasonable to conclude, that had there been suffering slaves in the hands of the rich, their cries must have been heard in Heaven, and also regarded in the denunciations delivered by the inspired apostle.

Persons who were in a state of abject poverty were under the necessity of devoting themselves to the service of the rich for wages, and that in many instances, during the space of several years together; and when they entered into a contract of such duration, they were bound to fulfil the term of service if required; and thus they were under the yoke; and when they bound themselves to the service of ill-disposed masters it became a grievous yoke; but, nevertheless, they were generally obliged to bear it until their term of service was completed according to agreement. Some in consequence of being in debt sold themselves for a limited time in order to make payment; other insolvent debtors might be sold by their creditors; and we may suppose some sold for crime. In addition to these, we may also suppose that many were bound as apprentices. All these several classes were under the yoke during the time for which they were bound to service; and therefore might be properly addressed in the language of Paul. 'Let as many servants as are under the yoke count their own masters worthy of all honor, that the name of God and his doctrine be not blasphemed. And they that have believing masters, let them not despise them.' That the apostle addressed servants, and not slaves, appears evident when we consider that God long before, positively prohibited the enslaving of his people, and with the prohibition he assigned the reason on which it was founded; 'They are my servants.' This reason must stand alike good in every age, and ever prohibit Christians from enslaving their brethren. 'But over your brethren — ye shall not rule — with rigor.' 'For they are my servants.' (Lev. xxv. 42, 46.) I cannot believe that the apostle under the inspiration of the Holy Spirit did, in opposition to this positive command, permit Christians to hold their brethren as slaves for life, and also to have the power of selling both them and their offspring as mere property! But it would be proper for the several classes of servants we have mentioned to fulfil their terms, and render the service due to their own masters, whether Christian or heathen. And to the heathen they ought to be both faithful and respectful, lest they should cause them to say that Christianity made their servants dishonest, or unwilling to render them such service and regard as were justly due. And love to their Christian masters, who were faithful and beloved brethren, ought to induce them to render them still more willingly the service and honor which were justly due ; and thus while fulfiling their just obligations, they would be doing good to their brethren, and so would enable them to extend their liberality to those who were propagating the gospel. And I do not see why all the addresses made to servants in the apostolic epistles might not be applicable to persons bound to servitude for a limited time. Such as were bound to intolerate heathen might endure great evils ; in such cases it would be desirable to be liberated by satisfying the master in some lawful way for the service due him. And, perhaps it was on this account that Paul said, 'Art thou called, being a servant, care not for it; but if thou mayest be free, use it rather.' But when this could not be obtained in an equitable manner, it would be their duty to serve even the froward as well as the gentle — it was such service as justice required ; hence, it was proper to enjoin obedience upon them. 'Servants, obey in all things your masters according to the flesh ; not with eye-service, as men-pleasers, but in singleness of heart fearing God.' (Col. iii. 22.) This plainly implies that the service was justly due ; and that, therefore, it should be rendered in the fear of God, who would punish them in case they should defraud their masters. And these same masters were commanded to give unto their servants whatever wages were due for their services. 'Masters, give unto your servants that which is just and equal.' (Col. iv. 1.) But in some instances, reference is made to the stripes which servants endured. And from this Mr. Cameron concludes such servants were slaves for life; but many who were servants for a limited time have endured stripes. Hence, enduring stripes is no certain proof of the existence of perpetual slavery. Again Mr. Cameron attempts, on page 21, to prove by the Greek phrase, O PAIS MOU, that the Centurion's servant whom our Lord healed was a slave born in his family; but the word pais is sometimes used as doulos, a servant. (Luke, i. 54.) 'He hath holpen his servant Israel.' (Luke xv. 20.) 'And he called one of the servants.' Pais is used in both those passages to signify servant. Hence the phrase, o pais mou, signifies 'my servant,' just as it is expressed in our translation. (Luke, vii. 7.) Therefore it has no reference to the servant being born in the Centurion's family, nor does it afford any evidence that he was a slave for life.

I have now considered the principal arguments which Mr. Cameron has adduced to prove that the apostles did permit the primitive Christians to hold slaves; and though I readily grant that they are the best his cause will admit, yet I do not think them sufficient to establish his point, or to justify his practice of holding as property his fellow-men. I am fully persuaded that a point so unreasonable, and a practice so unjust, can never find support from the sacred volume.

I have now completed my examination of the principal arguments which the abettors of slavery have drawn from the scriptures in order to support our modern system of cruel oppression.

You may expect me in my next to show that the scriptures do condemn the practice of slavery.

ADIEU.

LETTER XIII.

Dear Brother:

I shall now present to your consideration several passages of the sacred scriptures which I believe to be decidedly opposed to the kind of slavery which exists in our slaveholding States.

The first I shall invite you to consider is a prediction found in Gen. xv. 14. 'That nation whom they shall serve will I judge, and afterward shall they come out with great substance.' This prediction relates to the slavery which the Egyptians inflicted upon the descendants of Abraham. And for such infliction God said he would judge them; but if it be not unjust to enslave our fellow-men, why did the Almighty denounce sentence of judgment against the Egyptians for enslaving the nation of Israel? And why did he execute that sentence by inflicting upon them ten most desolating plagues? What were the disgusting plagues of bloody fountains, croaking frogs, loathsome and devouring insects and horrible diseases, but so many different emblems of the divine abhorrence of the crime of inflicting slavery upon an innocent nation? What were the plagues of massy hail-stones, terrific fire, and tremendous thunder, of horrible darkness, and of the destroying angel, the messenger of sudden death to all the first-born of Egypt, but the emblems of divine indignation against the injustice of slavery? Surely the various punishments inflicted upon the Egyptians for enslaving the Israelites are so many demonstrations that the practice of slavery is a crime of the greatest magnitude, and as such highly offensive to Jehovah. The great substance which the prediction awarded to the nation of Israel is likewise a striking demonstration of the injustice of enslaving the human species. The Egyptians did not escape with merely suffering severe inflictions of punishment; but they were made to remunerate the Israelites for the service which they had unjustly exacted from them. Hence, according to the prediction, the nation of Israel came out of Egypt 'with great substance.' Let it not be said that the Israelites were the chosen people of God, and that, therefore, to enslave them was peculiarly criminal. There could be no more natural injustice in enslaving them than there is in enslaving any other innocent people. And let it be remembered that God has given to his Son 'the heathen for his inheritance, and the uttermost parts of the earth for his possession.' (Psalm, ii. 8.) Then all nations are now the property of the Son of God, and consequently to enslave any of them must be as criminal as it was to enslave the nations of Israel. Permit me here to remark that the crime of the Egyptians in enslaving the Israelites was in several respects less aggravated than is that of the Americans in enslaving the Africans. The Egyptian slavery was much less rigorous than is that which exists in our slaveholding States. The Israelites were not made the property of individuals, as are the Africans in America — consequently they were not liable to be taken from their families and sold in the markets like beasts, nor does it appear that the females were at all enslaved; but that merely the males were made to labor under task-masters, in the service of the king. They were permitted to live in a body together, and to hold property; they had elders or rulers among them whom they could convene together when necessary; and according to their own testimony they were plentifully fed. These statements are fully verified by the book of Exodus ; and they show that the slavery to which the Egyptians subjected the Israelites was much more tolerable than is that to which the Africans are now subjected by the Americans. Hence in this respect the crime of the Egyptians was less heinous than is that of the American slaveholders, who alike enslave male and female, make them private property, separate them from their dearest relatives, and without regard to age or sex, buy and sell them in the markets as though they were beasts. And in many instances, they are made to endure nakedness and hunger. It is true that Pharaoh devised a cruel method of preventing the increase of the Israelites ; but it does not appear to have been executed to any considerable extent, and even that device, dreadful as it was, fell far short of the cruelty of subjecting men to a whole life of the severe torture, excessive toil and starvation, to which thousands of the Africans are subjected in various parts of the United States. Better far, for many of the hapless Africans to have entered the world under the bloody decree of Pharaoh, to have died by it, in an infantile state, than to endure a whole life of death under American bondage. It is undeniable, that in every slaveholding State many slaves endure sufferings immensely more dreadful than were those inflicted upon the new-born infants of Israel by the bloody command of Pharaoh. Hence, when the slavery of Egypt is viewed even in its worst forms, it does not appear to equal in cruelty that which exists among us. Consequently, it appears to me that the criminality of modern slavery does far exceed that of the slavery of Egypt.

I think it is proper to remark further, that at the time in which the Israelites were enslaved by the Egyptians, the knowledge of the natural rights of man was very limited, and of course despotism pervaded the world. The Egyptians were doubtless very ignorant in respect to the injustice of enslaving the Israelites, and although this did not free them from crime, yet it tended to the mitigation of their guilt ; but there has been no period in which the natural rights of man have been better understood than they are at this age, nor are they generally so well understood in the present time by any other nation as they are by the United States of North America, in which experience has proved the truth of theory in relation to both civil and religious liberty. Hence, we conclude that slavery never was in any other age attended with so high a degree of criminality as it is in the present ; nor is the crime of it in any other nation attended with so many aggravations as it is in our own. Consequently, if the crime of slavery in Egypt was great, it is immensely greater in America !

The second passage of Scripture I shall present to your consideration, is found in Exodus xxi. 16. 'He that stealeth a man and selleth him, or if he be found in his hand, he shall surely be put to death.' This law is recognized and re-sanctioned by the apostle Paul, (1 Tim. i. 9, 10.) 'The law is not made for the righteous man, but — for men-stealers.' It is evident that there is no method of introducing innocent men into a state of slavery, that is more just than that of stealing them. The criminality of stealing does not consist in the secret manner in which it is effected, but in the unjust violation of another's right. Hence, it is evident that the law against man-stealing forbids alike every other method of enslaving the innocent. I admit that a man by crime may forfeit his own right to liberty, but such forfeiture cannot justly take away the liberty of his offspring. Consequently, hereditary and involuntary slavery cannot possibly exist but by the violation of natural and unforfeited rights, and of course by the violation of the law which prohibits man-stealing. The very design of giving such a law was undeniably that of securing to innocent persons the natural right of freedom. I presume you will not imagine that the man who raises another has a right to his services during his life. Thousands of hapless orphans, without the means of support, are providentially cast upon society; but who will pretend that they who raise them, are entitled to their services during their lives, and therefore may justly enslave them? The service of a person until he arrives at the age of twenty-one years, is considered by the laws of our nation the price of his raising. Such service parents are allowed to receive for raising their children. And certainly slaveholders who raise Africans cannot be justly entitled to longer service. Indeed most, if not all of them, according to the plainest principles of justice, are not entitled to a moment's service from the Africans they raise. They generally bring them up in a very coarse manner, have not the trouble of nursing them, give them no education, and at the same time receive such labor from their parents as more than compensates for the little expense incurred by supporting them during their minority. Hence there are very few if any cases at all, in which slaveholders are justly entitled to the services of African children until they become twenty-one years of age, and surely much less are they entitled to the services of any of them during life. Consequently, from well established principles, it is evident that the man who enslaves another merely because he has raised him, violates his rights as much as the man-stealer does those of the man he steals and enslaves. But perhaps you may even suppose that they who purchase slaves have a just title to their offspring, and of course may enslave them without the violation of natural rights. But it ought to be recollected that the slaves who are thus purchased were themselves unjustly enslaved — they were either stolen or they descended from those who were stolen, and therefore none can have any right to buy or sell them. But were the parents justly bound to service during life, even that could not give the right of enslaving the offspring. It is admitted by all enlightened nations, that parents have no right to the service of their own children beyond a limited time, and therefore they are neither permitted to hold them in perpetual bondage themselves, nor to sell them for slaves during life. And certainly if parents, who generate, bear, and nurse children, have no right to hold slaves during life, no others can have such right. It cannot be even pretended that slaveholders have as much right to the service of children whom they have neither generated, borne, nor nursed, as parents have to those of their own offspring. If generating, bearing, and nursing a man cannot give the right of perpetual property in him, nothing else short of creating him can. Hence we conclude, with the utmost certainty, that the practice of our kind of of slavery, which originated in violence and theft, and is perpetuated by means equally unjust as those by which it had its origin, is a flagrant violation of the divine law against man-stealing. And it is worthy of remark, that the original word which the Apostle uses, (1 Tim. i. 10) and is translated into the word men-stealers, comprehends not merely those who steal men, but also all who are concerned either in enslaving any of the human species, or retaining them in slavery.* Indeed, it might be rendered slave-dealers with as much propriety as it is rendered men-stealers. And, in reality, there is no essential difference between these two classes of men ; both alike deprive innocent persons of their liberties : the one commits the theft, and the other consents to it, and receives and vends what is stolen. Now all slaveholders are in some degree concerned both in men-stealing and slave-dealing, and therefore the law is made for slaveholders as well as for men-stealers and slave-dealers. That they are all alike guilty to the same degree, I will not pretend to assert ; but that the most innocent and unsuspecting among them are 'partakers of other men's sins,' seems to me undeniable. And though 'they escape the judgment of men, yet they shall not escape the righteous judgment of God.' The sentence which God has annexed to the law against man-stealing, shows how much he abhors slavery. Death ! certain death ! is the penalty which the Almighty has attached to the crime of depriving an innocent person of his liberty. 'He that stealeth a man and selleth him, or if he be found in his hand, he shall SURELY BE PUT TO DEATH.' And it ought to be remembered that this awful penalty was annexed to the crime of enslaving the innocent at a period of the world when

* To this purpose is the following note, which was privately inserted in the Confession of Faith, revised A. D. 1805, by the General Assembly of the Presbyterian Church. ['1 Tim. i. 10. (The law is made) for whoremongers for them that defile themselves with mankind, for men-stealers. This crime among the Jews exposed the perpetrators of it to capital punishment. (Exodus xxi. 16.) And the apostle here classes them with sinners of the first rank. The word he uses in its original import, comprehends all who are concerned in bringing any of the human race into slavery, or detaining them in it. Hominum fures, qui servos vel liberos abducant, retinent, vendunt vel emunt. Stealers of men are all those who bring off slaves or freemen, and keep, sell, or buy them. To steal a freeman, says Grotius, is the highest kind of theft. In other instances we only steal human property, but when we steal or retain men in slavery, we seize those who, in common with ourselves, are constituted by the original grant lords of the earth. (Gen. i. 28.) Vid. Poli synopsin in loc.']

the ignorance of the rights of man tended much to mitigate the guilt of slavery. The criminality of slavery continually increases with the progress of knowledge.

The third passage I shall invite you to consider is found in Deut. xxiii. 15, 16. 'Thou shalt not deliver unto his master the servant which is escaped from his master unto thee. He shall dwell with thee, even among you, in that place which he shall choose in one of thy gates, where it liketh him best: thou shalt not oppress him.'

In this passage we have the judgment of God against one kind of servitude; the justice of the command necessarily supposes the injustice of the servitude to which it refers. And be that kind of servitude what it might, I am sure it could not be worse than that which is involuntary and perpetual; therefore the divine decision against it must be equally against that which exists in modern times. This divine decision originated in the principles of justice and mercy, and, of course, must be as immutable as are the principles in which it had its origin. Justice and mercy can never cease to require the protection of those who fly to us from oppression. Hence we conclude that the passage under consideration does fully condemn the modern practice of slavery.

The fourth passage I shall present to your consideration you will find in Isaiah lviii. 6. 'Is not this the fast that I have chosen? To loose the bands of wickedness, to undo the heavy burdens, and to let the oppressed go free, and that ye break every yoke.' That the Israelites did attempt the practice of involuntary and perpetual slavery is evident from Jer. xxxiv. 8, 17. In this they transcended the limits of divine permission in relation to servitude. Hence they were commanded 'to let the oppressed go free, and — break every yoke.' And if it was criminal in them to extend servitude beyond the limits of divine permission, it must be equally so in us. There is no divine permission for enslaving the Africans, and therefore the command is as obligatory upon their enslavers as it was upon the mancipating Israelites. Hence every slaveholder is commanded to break the yoke of bondage, and 'to let the oppressed go free.'

The fifth and last passage I shall present to your consideration contains the substance of the law and the prophets. It is found in Matt. vii. 12. 'Therefore all things whatsoever ye would that men should do to you, do ye even so to them: for this is the law and the prophets.'

Every man who is acquainted with the attendant and consequent evils of slavery would, if a slave, desire to be liberated. And certainly such desire would be consistent with the divine law. Hence, no man can hold an innocent person to involuntary servitude without violating the Savior's law of love. For in doing this he does to another what he would not wish another to do to him. No earthly consideration could induce the slaveholder to take the place of his slaves. Therefore it is abundantly evident that he does not do to them as he would have them do to him. He does hold them to service to which he would not wish himself to be held. There is no way of evading the force of these conclusions, but by first limiting the Savior's injunction to lawful desires, and then asserting that it is unlawful for a slave to desire to be free — consequently we find many adding 'like circumstances' to the text, in order to make it tally with their own conduct. I readily admit that the injunction necessarily supposes that we are bound to desire of others nothing but what is in accordance with the divine law; but nothing, except a mind under the infatuating influence of an insatiable avarice, can imagine that it is unlawful for a slave to desire freedom. All men were alike 'created free;' and for a man to desire what is his natural and unforfeited right, never can be discordant with the law of God. Hence Paul, when addressing servants, says, 'If thou mayest be free, use it rather.' Now this, whether it has reference to mere servants or involuntary slaves, proves that the desire for freedom is lawful, and that it is even a duty to obtain liberty when it is attainable. But perhaps you may ask, is it lawful for a slave to desire the master who has purchased him to liberate him with the loss of the purchase money? I say it is lawful. None have a right to sell a man who has never forfeited his liberty, and of course none can have a right to purchase him; and if a man has no right to purchase another, he has no right to hold him when purchased. And it is easier for a man to endure the loss of a few hundred dollars, than it is for one to endure a whole life of bondage. Hence we say, when one man holds another in bondage during life merely because he has given a few hundred dollars for him, he gives the most decisive evidence that he does not love him as he does himself. The slaveholder would give a million of dollars if he had them, rather than be a slave during life; yet for the sake of a few hundred he will hold another in slavery during life, and at the same time profess to love him as he does himself! But how absurd is such a profession! Could the most malignant hatred do worse than hold a man in abject slavery for life? Thus it is most evident that the slaveholder does violate the law and the prophets. And the New Testament is but a development of the principles contained in the law and the prophets. Hence the whole Bible is opposed to slavery. The sacred volume is one grand scheme of benevolence. Beams of love and mercy emanate from every page, while the voice of justice denounces the oppressor, and speaks his awful doom!

Finally, I shall consider some of the excuses which have been offered for the practice of slavery.

I. It is said 'the government has enslaved the Africans, and therefore slavery is the sin of the nation, and not of individuals.' Nothing can be more fallacious than this excuse. The government never made nor held a single slave, nor did it ever compel a single individual to become a slaveholder. Individuals first made, and still continue to hold slaves, and for these purposes they sought and obtained permission and protection from government. Hence they involved both themselves and the government in the guilt of slavery. Therefore it is as unjust as it is vain for slaveholders to charge their sin upon the government. Every one of them shall bear his own sin.

II. It is said, 'the laws of the slaveholding States prohibit the liberation of the slaves, and therefore the crime of slavery falls upon the States, and not upon individuals.' To this I reply, that those States did not compel any to become slaveholders, and therefore individuals stand first in the list of crimes. And besides this slaveholders made the very laws which prohibit emancipation, and they are the very men who prevent the repeal of those laws. Hence, they are the sole cause of the evil. It is vain for us to charge our sins upon the government which we made ourselves, and may alter when we please. And we may further add, that they who wish to liberate their slaves may give them a pass, and send them into other states whose laws will free them.

III. It is said, 'Alas! poor creatures, freedom

would ruin them; they are not capable of doing for themselves; they would all either starve or steal.'

Immaculate tenderness! Astonishing sympathy! But what is to be dreaded more than such tenderness and sympathy? Who would wish to have them exercised upon himself? The assertion that 'they are not capable of doing for themselves' is false, as may be shown by a thousand instances. Were not the Haytiens once in a state of the most abject slavery? Did they not liberate themselves? And have they not honorably maintained their independence, in spite of the powerful efforts of the French nation to subdue them? Have they not formed a respectable republican government? Have they not made wise regulations for the promotion of science among them? And have they not the prospect of becoming an enlightened and happy nation? And have not many of those who have been emancipated in America become wealthy and good citizens? And where shall we find any instances of starvation among them? Have not the poorest economists among them been able to provide something better than the few pints of corn per week in many places allowed to slaves? How many of them have gone entirely naked? And where have they committed worse thefts than have been committed by the whites? And is it not well known that many of the crimes charged upon the Africans have been perpetrated by white men? It appears to me undeniable, that freedom with its worst consequences, is better than slavery with its best consequences. The most miserable of those who are free, are not so miserable in every respect as are some in slavery. Hence, we say that the tenderness which induces men to hold others in abject slavery, in order to save them from the ruinous effects of freedom, is but a mere palliative for a guilty conscience, and must be the offspring of blind avarice.

IV. It is said 'that some slaves have very cruel masters, and therefore it is an act of benevolence in the humane to buy and hold them in bondage, in order to better their condition.'

This is a very plausible excuse for the practice of slavery, and has no doubt had a powerful influence upon many well-meaning people ; but it is as false as it is plausible. Every man readily supposes himself to be humane ; hence every man upon the same principle would think himself authorized to purchase and hold slaves, and thus the widest door would be opened to the practice of what we admit to be in itself unjust. If all the humane would refuse to hold slaves, the evil of slavery would soon be banished from the world. The example of the humane encourages the cruel by giving countenance to their oppressions ; and their kindness to their slaves keeps out of view many of the worst evils of slavery, and causes it to assume a mild and tolerable aspect ; thus their partial benevolence becomes universal cruelty. If slavery is unjust, it must be criminal to sanction it by our example.

Again, suppose you were to purchase from the Algerines an unfortunate captive whom they were determined to enslave during life, do you suppose that their determination to deprive him of liberty would justify you in subjecting him to similar bondage with some mitigations of suffering ? Certainly you would never so much as think of subjecting such a person to slavery for life unless his skin were black. But the color of the skin does not in the least alter the nature of the case; the law of love knows no distinction in colors ; it binds us alike to regard the natural rights of all men ; whatever is naturally due from us to a white man, is equally so to one that is black.

V. It is said, 'that the Africans are in slavery, and will certainly be continued in it, and therefore one may as well hold them as another ; and he who holds them does not take away their liberty, for this they never possessed.'

Suppose a man were to happen with a band of robbers, and they should invite him to join them in robbing a travelling gentleman of his money. He at first expostulates with them about the cruelty and injustice of robbery — they tell him he may have his choice as to the matter in question, but they are determined to have the traveller's money. He at length says — Alas! poor man, they will certainly take his money, and my refusing to take part with them will not alter the case, nor better the condition of the unfortunate stranger ; therefore I may as well join and get a share of the spoil — I may as well have it as another. Away he goes with the rest, and takes his share of the money. Is he the less guilty because the others would certainly have committed the robbery without him ? Then surely a man is not the less guilty in holding an innocent person in bondage, because he would certainly be held in it by another. An innocent man has ever a right to freedom, and therefore whoever holds him in bondage does take away his liberty.

VI. Finally, it is said, 'It will not do to free them among us. If they must be among us, let them be slaves.'

We are commanded to 'do justly and love mercy,' and this we ought to do without delay, and leave the consequences attending it to the control of Him who gave the command. We ought also to remember that no excuse for disobedience will avail us any thing when he shall call us to judgment. If we refuse to do the Africans justice, we may expect the supreme Governor of the world to avenge their wrongs, and cause their own arm to make them free! Hence, our own safety demands their liberation. Hold them in bondage, and you will inure them to hardship and prepare them for the day of battle. You will also keep them together, increase their numbers, and enable them to overpower the nation. Their enormous increase beyond that of the white population is truly alarming. But liberate them and their increase will become proportionate to the rest of the nation. They will scatter over this Union — many of them will emigrate to Hayti and Africa. Prepare them for citizenship, and give them the privileges of free men, and they will have no inducements to do us harm; but persist in oppressing them, and ruin will eventually burst upon our nation. The storm is gathering fast — dismal clouds already begin to darken our horizon. A few more years and the work of death will commence!

Now, my dear brother, I think I have clearly shown that both reason and revelation do condemn the practice of slavery. I therefore entreat you to liberate the poor Africans you have purchased, and provide for them some comfortable way of living. To have done this will give you no painful sensations upon a dying bed.

I must now close my series of letters. I hope you will receive them as so many tokens of sincere affection for you. My heart fills as I approach the closing moment. It seems as if I am about to bid you a long and uncertain farewell! All the tender scenes of our youthful days seem at once to rise to view, to awaken the softest sensibilities of nature, and excite the strongest solicitude for your happiness; while the appalling thought presses upon me that you will refuse to hear a brother's voice, the voice of reason, and what is infinitely more, the voice of God. A brother pleads with you; nature by all her tenderest sensibilities, and the God of nature, by all those heavenly sympathies that issued from a Savior's bleeding heart, plead with you to 'do justly, to love mercy,' 'and to let the oppressed go free!' And can you refuse? And if you do, I am your brother — I will not speak your doom!

FAREWELL.

THE END.

STANDARD ANTI-SLAVERY BOOKS

FOR SALE BY

ISAAC KNAPP,

NO. 25 CORNHILL, BOSTON.

APPEAL, in favor of that class of Americans called Africans, by Mrs. Child, a work which throws a flood of light on the subject of slavery, colonization, &c. Enriched with many rare and interesting anecdotes, and adorned with engravings. 12mo. pp. 216. Price 37½ cents single, $33.33 per hundred.

BOURNE'S PICTURE OF SLAVERY IN the U. S. 10 engravings. A book made up of facts which fell under the writer's own observation, illustrating abominations in the South. 18mo. pp. 228. Price, bound, 50 cents single, $37.50 per hundred.

CHARLES BALL, a story told by himself of a man who lived 40 years in Md., S. C. and Ga., as a slave under various masters, giving an account of the manners of the planters, and the condition and treatment of the slaves, with the perils and sufferings of a slave who twice escaped from the cotton country. A narrative of uncommon interest. 12mo. pp. 517. Price $1.25 single, $1 by the hundred.

GEORGE THOMPSON IN AMERICA. Letters and addresses during his residence in the U. S. from Oct. 1834, to Nov. 1835. 8vo. pp. 126. Price 37½ cents single, $30 per hundred.

GEORGE THOMPSON'S RECEPTION IN Great Britain, 18mo. pp. 238. Price 37½ cents single, $33.33 per hundred.

GEORGE THOMSON'S LECTURES AND Debates in England. 12mo. pp. 190. Price 50 cents single, $44 per hundred.

GODWIN ON SLAVERY, a valuable work by the well-known author of the treatise on Atheism. 12mo. pp. 258. Price 62½ cents single, $56 per hundred.

GUSTAVUS VASA, written by himself. The life of a native African, who was 'stolen out of his own land,' lived as a slave in Pennsylvania, went several voyages to the W. I. and Europe, and passed through a variety of wonderful scenes which give his narrative an interest scarcely surpassed by Robinson Crusoe ; with two fine lithographic prints. 12mo. pp. 294. Price 62½ cents single, $56 per hundred.

JAY'S INQUIRY into the nature and tendency of the American Colonization and Anti-Slavery Societies, 4th edition. This masterly collection of facts and arguments is unanswerable. 12mo. pp. 206. 37½ cents single, $33.33 per hundred.

LECTURES OF GEORGE THOMPSON, with a full report of the discussion between Mr. Thompson and Mr. Borthwick, the pro-slavery agent, held at the Royal Amphitheatre, Liverpool, Eng., and which continued for six evenings with unabated interest: compiled from various English editions. Also, a brief history of his connection with the Anti-Slavery cause in England. By Wm. Lloyd Garrison, Boston. 12mo. pp. 190. Price 50 cents single, $44 per hundred.

"NEGRO PEW"—an inquiry concerning the propriety of *distinctions in the house of God* on account of color. 18mo. pp. 108. 25 cents single, $22 per hundred.

PHILLIS WHEATLEY ; the memoir and poems of one who was a native African and a slave. With a beautiful lithographic likeness. Modern edition, 18mo. pp. 110. 37½ cents single, $30 per hundred.

POEMS written during the progress of Abolition in 1830–38, by J. G. Whittier. Embellished with a beautiful London copperplate engraving. 37½ cents single, $30 per hundred.

Recommended Reading

Beyond the River
The Untold Story of the Heroes of the Underground Railroad
by Ann Hagedorn

His Promised Land
The Autobiography of John P. Parker, former slave and conductor on the Underground Railroad
by John P. Parker

Freedom Light
Underground Railroad stories from Ripley, Ohio
by Edith M. Gaines

The Conductor
The Story of Rev. John Rankin,
Abolitionist's Essential Freedom Fighter
by Caleb Franz

www.ingramcontent.com/pod-product-compliance
Ingram Content Group UK Ltd.
Pitfield, Milton Keynes, MK11 3LW, UK
UKHW042014190726
13854UKWH00005B/2288